The Insanity Defense

ELGAR STUDIES IN LEGAL THEORY

Elgar Studies in Legal Theory is a series designed to cultivate and promote high quality works of scholarship on all aspects of legal theory. The focus of the series is on the development of original thinking in legal theory, with topics ranging from law and language, logic and legal reasoning, morality and the law, critical legal studies, and transnational law. Innovative work is encouraged from both established authors and the new generation of scholars.

Titles in this series include:

Gender, Alterity and Human Rights
Freedom in a Fishbowl
Ratna Kapur

Law and Evil
The Evolutionary Perspective
Wojciech Załuski

The Turning Point in Private Law
Ecology, Technology and the Commons
Ugo Mattei and Alessandra Quarta

The End of Law
How Law's Claims Relate to Law's Aims
David McIlroy

Domesticating Kelsen
Towards the Pure Theory of English Law
Alexander Orakhelashvili

Law in the First Person Plural
Perspectives from Rousseau
Bert van Roermund

Social Construction of Law
Potential and Limits
Michael Giudice

Law's Reality
A Philosophy of Law
Allan Beever

The Insanity Defense
A Philosophical Analysis
Wojciech Załuski

The Insanity Defense
A Philosophical Analysis

Wojciech Załuski

Professor of Law, Department of Philosophy of Law and Legal Ethics, Jagiellonian University, Krakow, Poland

ELGAR STUDIES IN LEGAL THEORY

Cheltenham, UK • Northampton, MA, USA

© Wojciech Załuski 2021

All rights reserved. No part of this publication may be reproduced, stored in a retrieval system or transmitted in any form or by any means, electronic, mechanical or photocopying, recording, or otherwise without the prior permission of the publisher.

Published by
Edward Elgar Publishing Limited
The Lypiatts
15 Lansdown Road
Cheltenham
Glos GL50 2JA
UK

Edward Elgar Publishing, Inc.
William Pratt House
9 Dewey Court
Northampton
Massachusetts 01060
USA

A catalogue record for this book
is available from the British Library

Library of Congress Control Number: 2021947349

This book is available electronically in the **Elgar**online
Law subject collection
http://dx.doi.org/10.4337/9781800379855

ISBN 978 1 80037 984 8 (cased)
ISBN 978 1 80037 985 5 (eBook)

Printed and bound by CPI Group (UK) Ltd, Croydon, CR0 4YY

In memory of my beloved Mum, Barbara Załuska

Contents

Introduction		1
1	The philosophical foundations of the insanity defense	16
	1 MODELS OF THE CRIMINAL RESPONSIBILITY OF THE MENTALLY ILL: A FIRST GLANCE	16
	2 CONCEPTIONS OF CRIMINAL RESPONSIBILITY	20
	2.1 The Incompatibilist Conceptions	21
	2.2 The Compatibilist Conceptions	25
	3 ACCOUNTS OF MENTAL ILLNESS	32
	3.1 The Affirmative Account	32
	3.2 The Negationist Account	34
	4 MODELS OF CRIMINAL RESPONSIBILITY OF THE MENTALLY ILL: A SECOND GLANCE	47
	5 THE PROBLEMS OF DEINSTITUTIONALIZATION	56
	6 EVALUATION OF THE MODELS	62
	6.1 Conceptions of Criminal Responsibility	62
	6.2 Accounts of Mental Illness	63
	7 Conclusions	67
2	The cognitive component	68
	1 TWO VARIANTS OF THE INSANITY DEFENSE	68
	2 THE INSANITY DEFENSE FROM A HISTORICAL PERSPECTIVE	68
	3 CONTROVERSIES OVER THE COGNITIVE COMPONENT	75
	4 PSYCHOPATHS AND THEIR NORMATIVE KNOWLEDGE	77
	4.1 The Nature of Psychopathy	77
	4.2 Arguments Against the Responsibility of Psychopaths	78

		4.3	Solutions to the Problem of the Responsibility of Psychopaths	82
		4.4	Psychopaths and Two Problems in Moral Psychology	88
	5	THE BORDERLINE BETWEEN BADNESS AND MADNESS		91
	6	CONCLUSIONS		101
3	The volitional component			103
	1	THE INTRICACIES OF THE CONCEPT OF WILL		103
		1.1	Will as a Decisional Power	103
		1.2	Will as a Post-decisional Power	111
		1.3	The Unity of Will	112
	2	THE OBJECTIONS TO THE VOLITIONAL COMPONENT		112
		2.1	The Epistemic Objection	113
		2.2	The Non-existence Objection	115
		2.3	The Slippery Slope and the Threat to Formal Justice Objection	117
	3	CONCLUSIONS		118
	4	FURTHER IMPLICATIONS: CRIMES OF PASSION		122
		4.1	The Case for Skepticism Towards Crimes of Passion	122
		4.2	Some Historical Remarks on Crimes of Passion	126
		4.3	Conclusions	128

Epilogue	130
Bibliography	132
Index	138

Introduction[1]

This book rests on the assumption that an in-depth analysis of the insanity defense (including the fundamental question of whether it is properly regarded as a legal defense) cannot be made without tackling the problems of philosophical anthropology, i.e., without asking some fundamental metaphysical questions about the nature of human agency or, more generally, about the nature of human beings.[2] Certainly, not all important questions that can be posed about the insanity defense will require forays into philosophical anthropology, but, as will be demonstrated in this book, the questions which do require such a treatment are numerous. Therefore, at the outset I deem it necessary to present the philosophical-anthropological view (picture) of human nature that will determine (more or less directly) my solutions to the questions that arise in the context of the insanity defense. However, prior to presenting this view, it is expedient to make some general remarks about the subject of my analysis: the insanity defense.

Along with automatism, involuntary intoxication, ignorance, entrapment, or duress, the insanity defense belongs to a specific group of legal defenses, viz. to excuses, which imply that even though the actions of an agent are considered to be bad, the agent himself – due to some fact about his mental state – cannot be held responsible for this act.[3] The group of excuses differs from the second group of legal defenses – that of justifications (including, e.g., self-defense or necessity), which imply that an agent can be held responsible

---

[1] The work on this publication was partly financed by the Priority Research Area Society of the Future under the program "Excellence Initiative – Research University" at the Jagiellonian University in Krakow.

[2] This kind of approach is by no means widespread in books devoted to the insanity defense. One title among the few exceptions is Michael Moore's excellent *Law and Psychiatry: Rethinking the Relationship* (1984). The structure of his argumentation (the defense of the legal view of persons as rational and autonomous against some psychiatric ideas: that badness is illness, that our mental life is ruled by the unconscious, and that the unity of self is a fiction) is very different from the one adopted in this book (although his "legal view of persons" is close to the personalist view defended in the present book).

[3] In the case of entrapment and duress, strictly speaking this is not some fact about the agent's mental state that excludes his responsibility, but some fact about the situation in which he found himself that made it extremely difficult for him to avoid acting wrongfully; but, in general, in the case of excuses, it is the mental state that counts.

for his *prima facie* bad act, but, due to some special circumstances of the act, this act can be justified, and therefore, on deeper reflection, cannot be regarded as bad (immoral/illegal) – indeed, it has become permitted or even obligatory.[4] Two additional remarks are in order here. First, I shall use the term "insanity defense" throughout this book even though it is hard to deny that, given the semantic associations of the adjective "insane," it may have some stigmatizing element. A possible alternative could be "the mental nonresponsibility defense." Yet in spite of its advantages: it is not stigmatizing and eliminates "the confusion as to whether retarded defendants who are not mentally ill are entitled to assert the defense" (Ellis, Luckasson 1985: 441), this felicitous term is still not well established in the relevant literature, so I shall stay with the traditional "insanity defense."[5] Secondly, the insanity defense should be distinguished from the mental competence required to stand trial. The insanity defense refers to the defendant's mental state at the time the crime was committed. If the defense is successful, then the defendant is found not guilty. By contrast, competence (or incompetence) to stand trial refers to the mental state of the defendant at the time when the trial is supposed to take place. If the defendant is found to be incompetent, then the trial is delayed until he regains his competence. In general, for a defendant to be deemed competent, he must be able to understand the charges against him and to assist in his own defense. The two institutions are obviously intricately connected with each other but my analysis will focus solely on the insanity defense, making only occasional references to the institution of competence to stand trial.

Let me now pass on to a presentation of the philosophical-anthropological view underlying my examination of the insanity defense. I will not provide its justification in a systematic and in-depth manner as this would require the writing of a very different book; I will just state it explicitly and present several arguments in its favor. While I believe it to be correct, needless to say I am fully aware that many scholars are not inclined to share my opinion. Those who reject it may interpret my analyses as a kind of philosophical exercise aimed at delineating the consequences that a given picture of human nature has for the insanity defense. This kind of interpretation should be facilitated by the fact that my analyses will be pursued in a broader context, since I strive

---

[4] One should note that it is a controversial issue whether the justification refers to the agent or to his act. On many (perhaps most) occasions these two ways of conceptualizing justification are equivalent but one can easily imagine a situation in which an agent's reasonable but false belief (e.g., that someone wanted to kill him) justifies *him* (retrospectively, so to say), but not his act (since his act could not be treated as a permissible exception to some general, prohibitory rule).

[5] Yet it should also be noted that the term "insanity defense" is misleading if it is to include (as it does) defense by reason of mental retardation.

to reconstruct the consequences of not only the philosophical-anthropological picture which I endorse, but also the consequences of alternative pictures.

The picture that underlies my analyses can be described in different ways: as the libertarian, the non-reductionist, the humanistic, or, most aptly, *the personalist*. It is based on the assumption that humans are truly unique beings, essentially different from animals. In consequence, any talk of non-human animals which implies that human beings are "human animals" is highly misleading as it overlooks this uniqueness and creates the false impression that the difference between humans and animals is one of degree. How can this uniqueness be described? Let me start from the observation that it is only humans that are not "closed" in their concrete perceptions (which can be called "the first-level representations of the world"). Thanks to their capacity to use abstract notions, they create abstract representations of the world (which can be called "the second-level representations of the world"). This capacity creates, as one may call it, an "ontological crevasse" between themselves and the world, and thereby makes them fundamentally "detached from" the world. Accordingly, a human being can direct his attention beyond his immediate (concrete) perceptions: either towards the "inside" – the depth of his self, or towards what lies "outside" his immediate perceptions. It is this capacity that Ernst Cassirer (1972) meant when saying that a human being is *animal symbolicum*. This capacity underlies (or is constitutive of) a human being's most unique faculty – that of free will.

The faculty of free will can be defined in two equivalent ways, highlighting its different aspects. The first definition, which emphasizes its dispositional aspect, states that free will is autonomy – the capacity for self-determination in accordance with some hierarchy of values. The thought that human beings are capable of self-determination, that they are not determined by any "human nature," but can choose their own nature, was memorably expressed by Pico della Mirandola in *Oratio de dignitate hominis*:

> Statuit tandem optimus opifex, ut cui dare nihil proprium poterat commune esset quicquid privatum singulis fuerat. Igitur hominem accepit indiscretae opus imaginis at que in mundi positum meditullio sic est alloquutus: "Nec certam sedem, nec propriam faciem, nec munus ullum peculiare tibi dedimus, o Adam, ut quam sedem, quam faciem, quae munera tute optaveris, ea, pro voto pro tua sententia, habeas et possideas. Definita ceteris natura intra praescriptas a nobis leges coercetur. Tu, nullis angustiis coercitus, pro tuo arbitrio, in cuius manu te posui, tibi illam praefinies. Medium te mundi posui, ut circumspiceres inde commodius quicquid est in mundo. Nec te caelestem neque terrenum, neque mortalem neque immortalem fecimus, ut tui ipsius quasi arbitrarius honorariusque plastes et fictor, in quam malueris tute formam effingas. Poteris in inferiora quae sunt bruta degenerare; poteris in superiora quae sunt divina ex tui animi sententia regenerari." O summam Dei patris liberalitatem, summam et admirandum hominis felicitatem! Cui datum id habere

quod optat, id esse quod vellit ... Nascenti homini omnifaria semina et omnigenae vitae germina indidit Pater ... (Pico della Mirandola 2010: 35–44).[6]

Human nature is therefore "Prothean," as Pico della Mirandola himself wrote: It can assume different forms, depending on a man's decision. We can be what we want to be and so we are responsible for what we become. The second definition points at free will's active (agential) aspect: An agent can be said to have free will if, and only if, when choosing a given action *a* at a given moment *m*, he is not causally determined to choose *this* action (*a*), i.e., can choose (without positing any change in the "state of the world" preceding the moment of choice *m*) also a different action (*not-a*) at the moment *m*. This aspect is captured by the famous definition of free will/free choice (*liberum arbitrium*) provided by Thomas Aquinas: *Liberum arbitrium est causa sui motus: quia homo per liberum arbitrium seipsum movet ad agendum* (*Summa Theologiae*, I, q. 83, a.1).[7]

It should be stressed that this – personalist – view of human nature cannot be conclusively proved. I shall confine myself to invoking two arguments in

---

[6] English translation (by A.R. Caponigri):
At last, the Supreme Maker decreed that this creature, to whom He could give nothing wholly his own, should have a share in the particular endowment of every other creature. Taking man, therefore, this creature of indeterminate image, He set him in the middle of the world and thus spoke to him: "We have given you, Oh Adam; no visage proper to yourself, nor any endowment properly your own, in order that whatever place, whatever form, whatever gifts you may, with premeditation, select, these same you may have and possess through your own judgment and decision. The nature of all other creatures is defined and restricted within laws which We have laid down; you, by contrast, impeded by no such restrictions, may, by your own free will, to whose custody We have assigned you, trace for yourself the lineaments of your own nature. I have placed you at the very center of the world, so that from that vantage point you may with greater ease glance round about you on all that the world contains. We have made you a creature neither of heaven nor of earth, neither mortal nor immortal, in order that you may, as the free and proud shaper of your own being, fashion yourself in the form you may prefer. It will be in your power to descend to the lower, brutish forms of life; you will be able, through your own decision, to rise again to the superior orders whose life is divine." Oh unsurpassed generosity of God the Father, Oh wondrous and unsurpassable felicity of man, to whom it is granted to have what he chooses, to be what he wills to be! ... Upon man, at the moment of his creation, God bestowed seeds pregnant with all possibilities, the germs of every form of life (6-9).

[7] English translation (by the Fathers of the English Dominican Province): "Free-will is the cause of its own movement, because by his free-will man moves himself to act."

its favor (as already mentioned, its deeper justification would be a topic for a different book).

The first argument states that if free will – the central faculty of the person – did not exist, there would be no moral justification for the practice of blaming and praising us for our actions. It must be admitted, however, that this argument can be criticized on the grounds that it presupposes the claim that the practice requires such a justification and that only the assumption of free will can provide it (I shall return to this argument in Chapter 1). The second one hints at the close connection between rationality and freedom of will: If we assume that human beings are capable of making rational judgments (this assumption is less controversial than the assumption of freedom of will), then we must agree that they are endowed with free will; the possessing of one of the capacities requires the possession of the other. These two arguments can be found in this classical passage from Thomas Aquinas's *Summa Theologiae*:

> Homo est liberi arbitrii, alioquin frustra essent consilia, exhortationes, praecepta, prohibitiones, praemia et poenae. Ad cuius evidentiam, considerandum est quod quaedam agunt absque iudicio, sicut lapis movetur deorsum; et similiter omnia cognitione carentia. Quaedam autem agunt iudicio, sed non libero; sicut animalia bruta. Iudicat enim ovis videns lupum, eum esse fugiendum, naturali iudicio, et non libero, quia non ex collatione, sed ex naturali instinctu hoc iudicat. Et simile est de quolibet iudicio brutorum animalium. Sed homo agit iudicio, quia per vim cognoscitivam iudicat aliquid esse fugiendum vel prosequendum. *Sed quia iudicium istud non est ex naturali instinctu in particulari operabili, sed ex collatione quadam rationis; ideo agit libero iudicio, potens in diversa ferri.* Ratio enim circa contingentia habet viam ad opposita; ut patet in dialecticis syllogismis, et rhetoricis persuasionibus. Particularia autem operabilia sunt quaedam contingentia, et ideo circa ea iudicium rationis ad diversa se habet, et non est determinatum ad unum. *Et pro tanto necesse est quod homo sit liberi arbitrii, ex hoc ipso quod rationalis est* (*Summa Theologiae* I, q. 83, art. 1; emphasis added).[8]

---

[8] English translation (by the Fathers of the English Dominican Province):
Man has free-will: otherwise counsels, exhortations, commands, prohibitions, rewards, and punishments would be in vain. In order to make this evident, we must observe that some things act without judgment; as a stone moves downwards; and in like manner all things which lack knowledge. And some act from judgment, but not a free judgment; as brute animals. For the sheep, seeing the wolf, judges it a thing to be shunned, from a natural and not a free judgment, because it judges, not from reason, but from natural instinct. And the same thing is to be said of any judgment of brute animals. But man acts from judgment, because by his apprehensive power he judges that something should be avoided or sought. *But because this judgment, in the case of some particular act, is not from a natural instinct, but from some act of comparison in the reason, therefore he acts from free judgment and retains the power of being inclined to various things.* For reason in contingent matters may follow opposite courses, as we see in dialectic syllogisms and rhetorical arguments. Now particular operations are

In my view, the second argument is very cogent: Human rationality indeed cannot be separated from the power of will and its freedom. One could object to this claim by saying that one can easily imagine a rational agent, that is: responsive to reasons, capable of weighing and comparing them, of deliberating about ends to pursue, and of selecting proper means to realize these ends, who is not free. Indeed, it *might seem* that a rational agent could act deterministically: The whole process of perceiving reasons, grasping them, and acting on them could proceed according to inexorable causal laws. Yet, upon deeper reflection, this objection proves to be implausible – vulnerable to two serious counter-objections. The first counter-objection, in its weaker form, states that it cannot be claimed at the same time that man is *animal rationale* (whose fundamental distinction is thinking, which is an intentional and teleological process) and that materialistic naturalism (according to which thinking is essentially a causal-mechanical process) is true. Consequently, we have to choose between the image of man as *animal rationale* and materialistic naturalism. In its stronger form, the counter-objection not only points to the necessity to choose between materialistic naturalism and the image of man as *animal rationale*, but it also shows that materialistic naturalism is an inconsistent, self-defeating view. More specifically, it shows that although the naturalist's statement "materialistic naturalism is true" is not formally incoherent (i.e., is not internally contradictory), it is self-referentially incoherent, i.e., undermines itself, because in the light of what it preaches (materialistic naturalism), it is just the result of a series of causally connected events occurring in the brain. This gives rise to the obvious question: Why should we treat this statement seriously if – ultimately – its origins have nothing to do with reasons, i.e., with arguments put forward by the free mind to support a certain conviction?[9] The second counter-objection states that an essential feature of a rational agent is consciousness and self-consciousness. In fact, this feature is built into the above definition of rationality: It is hard to imagine that the very process of weighing (attaching weights to) reasons, comparing them, especially (which happens frequently) when these reasons are inconclusive (i.e., when they have this kind of character which excludes applying to them formal methods – rules of mathematics, logic, or probability), and grasping and being guided by them could proceed without the active participation of consciousness. And consciousness can hardly be separated from the will: The final decisions of what weight to assign to various reasons for action and what action to take belong

---

contingent, and therefore in such matters the judgment of reason may follow opposite courses, and is not determinate to one. *And forasmuch as man is rational is it necessary that man have a free will* (emphasis added).

[9] I develop this line of argumentation at great length in Załuski 2017.

to the prerogative of the will. This last point can be developed along the lines indicated by John Searle (2010: 123), who wrote about the subjective experience of three "gaps": between reasons for an action and a decision to take this action, between a decision what to do and performing the action, and between starting an action and carrying it through to a conclusion. In Searle's view, these three gaps "are all parts of a continuous causal gap of conscious voluntary action" (2010: 123) – they are the experiences "of thoughts and actions where we do not sense the decisions and actions as causally fixed by the antecedent conditions" (2010: 123). Obviously, one could try to argue that the gaps are not real but illusionary – and their illusion results from our insufficient knowledge of the antecedent causes which deterministically forejudge what decision and action is taken. But even though this objection cannot be falsified (one can always posit the existence of some unknown causes to be revealed by the future development of science), it is highly implausible. It remains in deep tension with our common intuitions (which strongly suggest – against determinism implying that the physical world is closed to any non-physical influences – that our consciousness, understood in a non-reductionist manner, is causally efficacious). It would also lead to the undermining of the very idea of human agency. Thus, determinism arguably has insurmountable difficulties in accounting for the very existence of consciousness and of the related fact of human rationality (humans' ability to grasp and be guided by reasons).

As already mentioned, the above-sketched picture of human nature can be called "humanistic." In describing it this way, I invoke one of the several meanings of the word "humanism," viz. as referring to the view which asserts that human beings occupy a distinguished place in the universe among other living beings owing to the fact that they are autonomous (in the sense that they have free will) and rational (in the sense that they are responsive to reasons and act on reasons, or at least have the capacity to act on reasons). Therefore humanism, at least in the Renaissance meaning of this term, rejects the claim that human beings are nothing more than physical systems whose behavior is strictly governed by deterministic laws (some additional aspects of humanism will be highlighted below). Since the agent who satisfies both conditions – freedom of will and rationality – is called "a person," this view of human being can also be called "personalist." I shall use this last term throughout the rest of this book since it lacks the ambiguity that the term "humanism" is burdened with; the latter is at times used also by scholars who reject one (or both) of the assumptions that are crucial for the classical account of the person (the account developed, for instance, by Thomas Aquinas, Emmanuel Mounier, or Karol Wojtyła/John Paul II, and adopted in this book), viz. that human beings have free will; and that there exist objective values which human beings strive to realize.[10] By way of summary, let me invoke the famous definition by Emmanuel Mounier, according to which a person is

> un être spirituel constitué comme tel par une manière de subsistance et d'indépendance dans son être; elle entretient cette substance par son adhésion à une hiérarchie de valeurs librement adoptées, assimilées et vécues par un engagement responsable et une constant conversion; elle unifie ainsi toute son activité dans la liberté et développe par surcroît, à coups d'actes créateurs, la singularité de sa vocation (Mounier 1936: 63).[11]

This is not a complete picture of the personalist view but sufficiently detailed at this stage of my considerations. But much more needs to be said about the will – as part of this picture. This will be done in Chapter 3, prior to making an analysis of the volitional component of the insanity defense. In summary, *it is an essential feature of the personalist view that it defines human being first and foremost in terms of reason and (free) will – his spiritual powers, rather than in terms of desires or instincts – his affective and instinctual side.*

Let me repeat that my analyses of the insanity defense will be more than just a matter of deriving conclusions from the above philosophical-anthropological assumptions. Above all, they will have a contextual character: I shall present my view of the insanity defense in the broader context of other views, based on different (philosophical-anthropological) assumptions (which I shall be presenting, though not in a systematic manner, throughout this

---

[10] The first assumption is rejected by what can be called *naturalistic* "humanism," having little in common with the original version of humanism defended, for example, by Pico della Mirandola. A good example is Michael Schimdt-Salomon's (2012) book *Manifest des evolutionären Humanismus*, in which he develops a doctrine he calls "evolutionary humanism." He understands this kind of humanism only in purely normative terms as a postulate of the "humanization" (improvement) of the living conditions of human beings. He does not regard the assumption of freedom and rationality as components of humanism. The view of man assumed by Schimdt-Salomon is in fact purely naturalistic. One can discern a related trend in understanding humanism among those thinkers who are motivated by the fascination of the technological achievements of human beings (their version of humanism can be called "Promethean humanism"). The second assumption was rejected by "existentialist humanism"; its representatives (e.g., Jean Paul Sartre) conceded that human beings are endowed with free will but denied the existence of objective values; in their view, values are not discovered but created by human beings.

[11] Translation (by the author):
a spiritual being constituted as such by his way of subsistence and independence of his being; he upkeeps this substance by his adherence to a freely adopted hierarchy of values, assimilated and lived by a responsible engagement and constant conversion; he unifies in this way his whole activity in liberty and, additionally, develops, by creative acts, this singularity of his vocation.

book). As already mentioned, this approach to the question of the insanity defense is based on the premise that there is a connection (a "bridge") between philosophical-anthropological assumptions and the views on the insanity defense. But how might one describe this connection in a more precise manner? The answer to this question is straightforward: The connection goes *via* conceptions of (moral and legal) responsibility. In other words, a given picture of human beings implies a certain conception of responsibility which, by itself or with some additional premises (especially, as we shall see, the premises determining the view of mental illness), influences the way in which we understand the responsibility of the mentally ill (insane). It is therefore pertinent to clearly indicate here what conception of responsibility is implied by – or is most naturally connected to – the personalist picture of human beings assumed in this book.

Most generally, it can be said that the personalist picture implies that free will is a necessary condition of responsibility (of a person P for committing an offence a). However, this description is somewhat vague as it allows three quite different "free will-based" conceptions of responsibility (i.e., such conceptions which imply that human beings have free will, and that free will is at least a necessary condition of responsibility).

According to the first one (the stricter), a person P is responsible for his action a if, and only if, P has free will and his action was undertaken in the absence of external coercion (of the so-called *vis compulsiva* or *vis absoluta.*)[12] The second (less strict) states that a person P is responsible for his action a if, and only if, P has free will and, in undertaking this action, he was free from both external and internal coercion. These two conceptions imply that responsibility is not gradable: Its ascription is an all-or-nothing question. The first conception is stricter because it assumes that free will is "activated" even among people whose actions are not fully voluntary, i.e., are not free from internal coercion (e.g., among the mentally ill). Let me note, *en passant*, that it is precisely this conception which was assumed by many of the adherents of the abolition of the insanity defense in some "conservative" states in the US (e.g., Idaho, Montana). The picture of human nature which they endorsed can be called *radically libertarian*: It assumes that free will is never "suspended" among the agents, and, consequently, it is as effective among the mentally ill

---

[12] An "action" done as a result of *vis absoluta* (one of two forms of external coercion), in which the decisional component is entirely absent (because an agent is physically forced to take a given "action"), is not an act in the strict sense. In the case of *vis compulsiva* (another form of external coercion) where the agent is faced with a threat and thereby coerced into choosing a "lesser evil," the decisional component is present. But he is forced to act, so to say, against himself, so responsibility ascription would be quite controversial in such a case (although the dispute on this issue is still ongoing).

as among the mentally sane. This conception is *radically libertarian* but it can hardly be called personalist: A truly personalist conception assumes a *less rigid* account of free will; *it stresses the uniqueness of human beings, but does not deny the fact that their unique faculties may sometimes fail to function properly* (this is another aspect of personalist humanism, which supplements those mentioned above). Thus, the second conception of responsibility is *personalist*: It prohibits blaming an agent for his actions which are not fully voluntary (i.e., which are not free from *both* external and internal coercion). This conception can be understood in two slightly different ways: We can say either that it implies that free will is "activated" only among those whose actions are fully voluntary (free from internal and external coercion), or that free will is always "active" (even among those whose actions are not fully voluntary) but it can ground an ascription of responsibility *only if* an action is fully voluntary.

Apart from the two above-mentioned "free will-based" conceptions, one can also distinguish the third one, which implies that (moral and legal) responsibility is a matter of degree: *It is proportional to our moral desert*, to what we do, thanks to our free will, with our character – our capacities and propensities that were "given" to us (by our genes or the environment), also taking into account the historical circumstances in which we act. This conception requires that we take some forms of moral luck into account when making ascriptions of responsibility, viz. character luck and situation luck. This conception, which is also (like the second one) justified by the personalist view of human beings,[13] was elegantly described by Clive Staples Lewis in the following passage:

> The bad psychological material is not a sin but a disease. It does not need to be repented of, but to be cured. And by the way, that is very important. Human beings judge one another by their external actions. God judges them by their moral choices. When a neurotic who has a pathological horror of cats forces himself to pick up a cat for some good reason, it is quite possible that in God's eyes he has shown more courage than a healthy man may have shown in winning the V.C. When a man who has been perverted from his youth and taught that cruelty is the right thing, does some tiny little kindness, or refrains from some cruelty he might have committed, and thereby, perhaps, risks being sneered at by his companions, he may, in God's eyes, be doing more than you and I would do if we gave up life itself for a friend. It is as well to put this the other way round. Some of us who seem quite nice people may, in fact, have made so little use of a good heredity and a good upbringing that we are really worse than those whom we regard as fiends. Can we be quite certain how we should have behaved if we had been saddled with the psychological outfit, and then with the bad upbringing, and then with the power, say, of Himmler? That is why Christians are told not to judge. We see only the results which a man's choices

---

[13] Though, it should be added that this conception is somewhat in tension with the radical understanding of self-determination, typical, for instance, of the above-quoted Pico della Mirandola.

make out of his raw material. But God does not judge him on the raw material at all, but on what he has done with it. Most of the man's psychological makeup is probably due to his body: when his body dies all that will fall off him, and the real central man, the thing that chose, that made the best or the worst out of this material, will stand naked. All sorts of nice things which we thought our own, but which were really due to a good digestion, will fall off some of us: all sorts of nasty things which were due to complexes or bad health will fall off others. We shall then, for the first time, see every one as he really was. There will be surprises (Lewis 2009: 91–92).

I apologize to the reader for this long quote, yet it perfectly encapsulates the spirit of the conception that will play some role in my further analyses (especially when dealing with the problem of responsibility of psychopaths in Chapter 2). This conception, which I term the "cosmic/God's eyes conception of responsibility," can be more precisely presented in the following way: A person P is responsible (blamable) for his action a if, and only if, P has free will and his action was fully voluntary (free from internal and external coercion), and his responsibility (blame) is a matter of degree: The easier it was for him (given his "psychological makeup") to refrain from doing a, the higher the degree of his responsibility for a.[14] Thus, according to this conception, what is of crucial importance is not the result or achievement but the moral effort to reach the result or achievement – the fact an agent has done the best he can with what he has at his disposal (his natural abilities and propensities).

Let me summarize: All three conceptions of responsibility are libertarian (in the sense that they are based on the assumption that free will is not an illusion), but only the last two can plausibly be called personalist. The question is: Which of these three conceptions is most plausible? The first one is *too* strict: It leads to blaming people who arguably should not be blamed (those whose actions were not fully voluntary); furthermore, it relies on the dubious descriptive assumption that free will functions in the same way among those whose actions are fully voluntary and those whose actions are not. Consequently, I assume that the second conception is an acceptable conception of moral and legal responsibility. It provides both a deep justification of punishment and, at the same time, can be practically realized by human beings. This last feature distinguishes it from the third conception, which may be, all things considered, the *right one* (as it arguably treats the idea of moral desert in a nuanced and proper way) but it cannot be realized by humans (hence the name I have given it here: "the cosmic/God's eyes").

---

[14] It seems that this conception, putting so much stress on moral desert/effort, could not have arisen without the influence of Christianity: In ancient ethical thought, the role of desert was not emphasized or marginalized (which was probably due to the fact that ancient thinkers did not know, or more precisely did not discover, the faculty of free will, without which the concept of moral desert loses its philosophical foundations).

What I have described so far are the two presuppositions of my analyses of the insanity defense, viz. the personalist picture of human beings and (the consequent) "free will-based" conception of responsibility, which states that free will *plus* full voluntariness are the necessary and jointly sufficient conditions of moral and legal responsibility. But how, in detail, will these analyses be carried out in this work? Their structure will be dictated by the fact that the insanity defense can be examined at two different levels. The first level concerns its most general assumption, viz. that the mentally sane can be held criminally responsible, and the mentally ill cannot (I shall call it the "Standard Model" of the criminal responsibility of the mentally ill). This assumption is common for all specific varieties of the insanity defense, which are distinguished according to a different criterion, viz. according to the *psychological content* of mental incompetence, which they recognize as releasing the accused from responsibility. The content may be narrow (thin) or broad (thick): It may embrace the cognitive component alone ("I did not know what I was doing," "I did not know that what I was doing was wrong") or also the volitional one ("I could not control my action, I could not refrain from making this action"), and each of these components can, in turn, be understood narrowly – less leniently/more restrictively – or broadly – more leniently/less restrictively. The narrow understanding of the structure of the insanity defense (confining it only to the cognitive component) and the narrow understanding of any of its components (excluding, e.g., "affective knowledge" from the cognitive test) are more restrictive (less lenient) towards offenders because they amount to providing less demanding conditions for responsibility ascriptions: They have the effect of heightening the threshold for a successful insanity defense and, consequently, of decreasing the number of offenders who can effectively invoke it during a trial (the threshold is highest if the structure of the defense is reduced to its cognitive component and this component is understood narrowly, and lowest if the defense includes both components understood broadly). Now, it is precisely the psychological content that constitutes the second level of analysis of the insanity defense. It is worth noticing that the first level is rarely distinguished in the relevant literature: The assumption that underlies the insanity defense – that only the mentally sane can be held morally responsible – usually appears to be taken for granted, and thereby not analyzed at great length if it is analyzed at all. But such an approach impoverishes the analysis of the insanity defense. It overlooks the fact that the criminal responsibility of the mentally ill can be – and in some jurisdictions *is* – regulated in a different way: Mental insanity is not always a legal excuse releasing the offender from criminal responsibility. Furthermore, even if all criminal justice systems assumed the insanity defense, it would still be necessary, if we wished to gain better understanding of it, to carefully trace its philosophical-anthropological assumptions (as well as the assumptions of the hypothetical other solutions to the problem of the criminal responsibility of the mentally ill).

These two levels of the analysis of the insanity defense can be easily discerned in the structure of this book. The task of identifying the philosophical assumptions of the Standard Model and other models of criminal responsibility of the mentally ill is undertaken in Chapter 1. I distinguish the models on the basis of two criteria: the mental state of the offender (mentally sane or mentally insane), and criminal responsibility (admitted or excluded). As a result, four main models are distinguished (variants of them are also analyzed in Chapter 1):

(M1 – *Standard*): Mentally sane → Responsible, Mentally insane → Not-responsible
(M2 – *Perverse*): Mentally sane → Not-Responsible, Mentally insane → Responsible
(M3 – *Negative Equalization*): Mentally sane → Not-Responsible, Mentally insane → Not-Responsible
(M4 – *Positive Equalization*): Mentally sane → Responsible, Mentally insane → Responsible

I shall try to provide a thorough analysis of their philosophical underpinnings, arguing that there are two main factors which determine the choice among them – the assumed conception of responsibility and the account they provide of mental illness. Accordingly, I shall supply a detailed analysis of various conceptions of responsibility (in addition to those which have been presented above) and of two accounts of mental illness (which I call "affirmative" and "negationist"). The analysis of these accounts is not purely theoretical; it also draws considerably on the history of 20th-century psychiatry, with a particularly detailed presentation of the anti-psychiatry of the 1960s. It was within this current that the "negationist" account was developed, and this work will examine its influence on the shaping of the institution of the insanity defense in various legal systems. In this chapter I advocate the already mentioned "free will-based" conception of criminal responsibility and an affirmative view of mental illness, which jointly justify the Standard Model of the criminal responsibility of the mentally ill, i.e., the insanity defense. Chapter 1 therefore answers the question of why the law should recognize the insanity defense at all. However, it does not say anything about the concrete shape that this type of defense should take, i.e., whether it should contain both components – the cognitive and the volitional – and, if so, how they should be understood (narrowly or broadly). This second level of the analysis of the insanity defense is developed in the remaining two chapters.

In Chapter 2, I first present various possible formulations of the cognitive component, drawing on the history of the insanity defense in various legal systems. I then pass to the analysis of the very notion of normative (moral and legal) knowledge (crucial for this component). This will lead me to the problem of the moral and legal responsibility of psychopaths. I formulate a critical analysis of various solutions to this problem proposed in the relevant literature and reject the following: that psychopaths can be held legally responsible but not morally responsible; that they cannot be held responsible either morally or legally; that they cannot be held morally responsible and can be held legally responsible but only for the so-called *mala prohibita*. I defend the following solution: Psychopaths can be held responsible both morally and legally (like all "normal," i.e., non-psychopath, offenders), and their specific features (e.g., their lack of – or at least deficits in – moral emotions and empathy) can only matter when we shift our ethical perspective and invoke the "cosmic/God's eyes" of moral responsibility. As mentioned before, I find two "free will-based" conceptions (the non-gradable one and the gradable one – the "cosmic/God's eyes") of moral responsibility plausible but in different contexts: While the first one is suitable for human moral judgment, the other one involves some "external" (supra-human, God's), more objective moral judgment as it is based on information which, in principle, is inaccessible to human beings. If we wanted to dispense with metaphysics or theology and limit ourselves to human moral judgment alone, we could say that the first conception must be invoked when we make "normal" moral judgments, while the second one may be proper in those moments in which we try to engage in a deeper ("cosmic/God's eyes") moral reflection. The typical result of this kind of deeper moral reflection is likely to be a stronger propensity to forgiveness since this reflection must be accompanied by ethical and intellectual humility, flowing from the awareness of our own sinfulness and from our limited access to information about the agents; this humility should lead to our interpreting all uncertain information in favor of the person being morally judged; only God or a "cosmic observer," knowing all the relevant information, will have the right to be a severe judge. But my claim that the specific features of psychopaths should be taken into account while "switching" to the "cosmic/God's eyes" conception of responsibility does not imply that their case is unique: The degree of the responsibility of all agents, whether psychopathic or not, will have to be properly accommodated to their "psychological makeups." It may, indeed, turn out that the features of psychopaths substantially decrease their responsibility; but we (as human beings) cannot know that. Equally it may emerge that the "psychological makeup" of many non-psychopathic agents is a more serious obstacle to moral behavior than that of psychopaths (although, let me repeat: If *human beings* engage in a moral reflection based on the "cosmic/God's eyes" conception of responsibility the typical results should be an increased readiness to forgiveness). In the course of my analysis of the responsibility of psychopaths I shall also examine the problem of the borderline between madness and extreme badness (evil), trying to answer the question of whether extreme evil can be imputed to agents or whether it should be regarded as a manifestation of their madness. I will distinguish five different senses of extreme evil: (1) doing evil just for the sake of doing evil; (2) sadistic wrongdoing, i.e., deriving pleasure from making the other person suffer; (3) doing evil for no intelligible reason; (4) doing non-natural evil, that is, violating the most elementary norms presumably inscribed in our nature by biological evolution, e.g., norms prohibiting us from killing our parents, siblings, children; and (5) doing beastly or brutish evil (in the sense of the Aristotelian *theriotes*) – evil that is absolutely horrifying for it resembles the actions of wild beasts. I shall argue that only the last three types of extreme evil, and especially type (3) and (5), can be regarded as madness, which means that there are types of extreme evil which can be committed by mentally sane people. Therefore, extreme evil, *ipso facto*, does not amount to madness.

In Chapter 3 I provide a critique of the volitional component, a critique which will have several layers. The most general one is connected with the personalist picture of human nature adopted in this book. The picture, as already mentioned, assumes that human beings are endowed with autonomy – the capacity for self-determination. This implies that they possess a certain faculty – will – and this faculty is understood as capable of resisting various internal and external influences. This understanding of will, assumed within the so-called classical tradition of philosophy and constituting an essential element of the personalist picture of man, implies that will is a *decisive* faculty of action; if it is "defeated," i.e., if an agent acts contrary to his will, then he can be blamed for it. The chapter provides a more detailed account of this understanding of will from a historical perspective, along with support for the claim that this personalist philosophical-anthropological conception casts more than a shadow of doubt on the volitional component of the insanity defense. However, my critique of this component is not only based on this conception. I formulate several other, more specific, objections against the inclusion of the volitional component into the insanity defense; I term them as follows: "the epistemic objection," "the non-existence objection," "the slippery slope objection," and finally, "the formal justice objection." This critique will not lead, however, to the rejection of the volitional component but rather to the postulate of its very restrictive or less lenient understanding. The chapter also traces the further implications of the critique of the volitional component of the insanity defense, viz. those regarding the so-called crimes of passion. I argue, drawing on my critical analysis of the volitional component of the insanity defense, that there are no cogent reasons to distinguish them as a separate category of crimes that deserve more lenient treatment.

1. The philosophical foundations of the insanity defense

1 MODELS OF THE CRIMINAL RESPONSIBILITY OF THE MENTALLY ILL: A FIRST GLANCE

The insanity defense is the standard (adopted in nearly all contemporary legal systems) model of the regulation of criminal responsibility of the criminal offenders who are mentally insane. It is based on the *prima facie* uncontroversial assumption that the mentally sane can be held criminally responsible, and the mentally insane cannot. This assumption in fact embraces two different claims: that the concept of mental illness/disorder is fully legitimate, and that mental illness/disorder (in conjunction with its psychological effects, which are certain mental – cognitive and/or volitional – incapacities or at least serious impairments of certain mental capacities) constitute an exculpatory circumstance or at least one mitigating the penalty for committing an offense.

Yet the very fact that this model is dominant (and thus why I call it "Standard") does not mean that none of its assumptions cannot or have not already been called into doubt. In fact, as already mentioned in the Introduction, one can distinguish four models of the regulation of the criminal responsibility of the mentally insane on purely logical grounds. The distinction is made on the basis of two criteria, namely mental state (mentally sane and mentally insane), and criminal responsibility (admitted, excluded):

> (M1 – *Standard*): Mentally sane → Responsible, Mentally insane → Not-responsible
> (M2 – *Perverse*): Mentally sane → Not-Responsible, Mentally insane → Responsible
> (M3 – *Negative Equalization*): Mentally sane → Not-Responsible, Mentally insane → Not-Responsible
> (M4 – *Positive Equalization*): Mentally sane → Responsible, Mentally insane → Responsible

M1 is the already mentioned Standard Model (the insanity defense): It treats the difference between the mentally sane and insane as relevant in the context of criminal responsibility. M2 also treats this difference as relevant but does so in an idiosyncratic, "perverse" manner: Mental sanity, not mental illness, is an exculpating circumstance. The other two models can be called "equalization models" since they regard the difference as irrelevant (or unfounded): M3 can be called the "Negative Equalization Model" because it assumes that neither the mentally sane nor the mentally insane can be held criminally responsible, whereas M4 can be called the "Positive Equalization Model" because it assumes that both can be held criminally responsible. It is interesting to note that M3 and M4 were endorsed by many philosophers and M4 was in fact adopted in some legal systems (as we shall see later in this chapter). M2 was neither defended philosophically nor adopted in legal systems – so it is distinguished here only for classificatory reasons. But it is worth noticing that one can distinguish a related model that was adopted (albeit rarely) in legal systems, viz. the model in which the mentally sane are held responsible for offenses they have committed, but the mentally insane are held *more* responsible for the same offenses, i.e., in which mental illness is an aggravating circumstance (I shall say a few more words about this model in Section 4 of this chapter).

The bulk of my analysis will be devoted to examining the philosophical foundations of the above models. I therefore attempt to present the Standard Model in a broader context by depicting other possible models of criminal responsibility of the mentally insane. The importance of providing such a context stems from the fact that the presuppositions of different models of criminal responsibility of the mentally sane have not as yet been presented in a systematic way in the relevant literature. This chapter is aimed at filling in this lacuna, which means that its main goal is analytical. I argue that the models are determined by two factors: the conceptions of criminal responsibility and the accounts of mental illness. However, the task of this chapter is not only analytical; I also provide arguments for the normative claim that the Standard Model is the optimal one (and that thereby it is not by chance that the model is "standard"). The arguments will, at least in part, appeal to the personalist view of human nature presented in the Introduction.

The outline of the chapter is as follows: Section 2 discusses the conceptions of criminal responsibility; Section 3 presents two different accounts of mental illness; Section 4 shows how these conceptions and accounts determine various models of the regulation of criminal responsibility of the mentally insane; Section 5 deals with the process of the so-called deinstitutionalization of mental illness; and Section 6 provides an evaluation of the models.

Before I move on to conduct my further analyses, three important remarks need to be made.

First, as we shall see in Section 2, not all models of the regulation of the criminal responsibility of the mentally insane are determined by both conceptions (of criminal responsibility and mental illness); some of the conceptions of criminal responsibility can justify a given model by themselves.

Secondly, the second dimension (an account of mental illness) is only relevant for the so-called "mixed" – psychiatric-psychological – account of mental incompetence (implied in the above description of the Standard Model) and within a "single" – *purely psychiatric* – account of mental incompetence.[1] It is clear that if one accepts a "single," *purely psychological* account (which dispenses with the very concept of mental illness/disorder), then it does not matter which conception of mental illness is assumed. Additionally, it should be noted that the *strength* of the relevance of a conception of mental illness is greater in the purely psychiatric model than in the mixed one, and how great this strength is in the mixed one will depend on how the relationship between mental illness/disorder and mental incapacities (psychologically defined) is exactly conceived: whether conceptually (in which case it is part of the definition of a mentally insane person that he has suffered, at least at the time of the criminal act, from mental illness/disorder), or, as one may call it, "diagnostically" or "evidentially" (in which case the fact that a person has suffered from a mental disease/disorder is not part of the concept of mental insanity but makes the hypothesis of the person's being mentally insane more probable). In the former case (which implies that a person who does not suffer from mental illness/disorder cannot be mentally insane) the relevance is stronger than in the latter case (which implies that a person who does not suffer from mental illness can be mentally insane).[2] This first interpretation, postulating the conceptual relation between mental illness/insanity and mental insanity, seems to be dominant in legal doctrine. I shall assume this interpretation throughout my further analyses. I discount here the complication which arises from the fact that, in many penal codes, e.g., in the Polish penal code, mental incompetence can also be caused by *mental deficiency/retardation*. When one takes into account this complication, one cannot, strictly speaking, say that there is a conceptual/definitional connection between mental illness/disorder/disturbance and mental insanity, though, of course, one can say that there is such a connection between mental illness/disorder/disturbance *or* mental deficiency/retardation on the one hand, and mental insanity on the other.

---

[1] Pure accounts are much less frequent than mixed ones; for instance, the purely psychiatric model was accepted only for a short time in the American legal doctrine, in the wake of the case of *Durham v United States* in 1954; the so-called Durham rule provided that a defendant is non-responsible if his unlawful act was "the product of mental disease or mental defect." I shall return to this solution in Chapter 2.

[2] The evidential understanding is close to the so-called reductionist thesis, which says that "there is not anything about a mental illness that makes it sufficient to excuse, and that mental illness excuses via ignorance or compulsion" (Reznek 1997: 152).

So, thirdly, I shall not analyze the problem of the moral and legal responsibility of the mentally deficient/retarded. There are, of course, many similarities between the situation of the mentally ill and the mentally deficient/retarded, but the differences seem to be at least equally numerous. For instance, the definitional feature of the mentally retarded is a low IQ (manifesting itself in perception, attention and linguistic deficits, problems with or incapacity of abstract thinking, learning problems, etc.), whereas the mentally ill (e.g., schizophrenics) usually have a normal IQ (as noticed by Ellis and Luckasson (1985: 427): "the irrationality, paranoia, and delusions that indicate mental illness and which are related to criminality are not indicators of mental retardation"). This difference seems to have far-reaching implications, e.g., for the analysis of the cognitive component of the insanity defense: One would have to conduct a separate analysis of this component for the mentally retarded. The volitional component would have to be analyzed separately as well: The mentally retarded are characterized by weakness of will, suggestibility (they are easily influenced by others as they have a strong need for contact with stronger personalities), impulsivity, and emotional immaturity.[3] Furthermore, mental illness usually has a dynamic character, whereas mental retardation is more static (it appears at birth or in early childhood and is in the overwhelming majority of cases permanent), which implies that legal policies addressed to the mentally ill (aimed at their curing) may be inadequate for the mentally retarded. Of course, it may happen that a person is at the same time mentally ill and mentally retarded (about 30 percent of the mentally retarded are mentally insane; cf. Ellis, Luckasson 1985: 425); but, generally speaking, the onset of mental illness is not correlated with the level of intelligence. Another problem is that the mentally retarded are a largely variable group: The concept of mental retardation ranges from borderline (IQ from 70 to 84 on the Wechsler scale) to profound (IQ under 24) – the intermediate levels are mild (55–69), moderate (40–45) and severe (25–39) mental retardation. However, on the other hand, although the concept of mental retardation seems very inclusive, it is much less fuzzy than that of mental illness. All those differences would have to be taken into account in a thorough analysis of the responsibility of the mentally retarded. The analysis might lead, for instance, to the conclusion that the volitional component, which I criticize in Chapter I as part of the insanity defense, should be allowed for in the case of the mentally retarded (especially if their intellectual impairments are profound, and thereby also likely to

---

[3] Although it should be added that "the best modern evidence suggests that the incidence of criminal behavior among people with mental retardation does not greatly exceed the incidence of criminal behavior among the population as a whole" (Ellis, Luckasson 1985: 426).

undermine their volitional capacities); furthermore, the mentally retarded are less likely to abuse the volitional component by invoking it *mala fide* in their defense. The problem of the responsibility of the mentally deficient/retarded would therefore require a separate examination, one which goes beyond the scope of this book.

2   CONCEPTIONS OF CRIMINAL RESPONSIBILITY

I shall use the term "criminal responsibility" in the general sense of accountability for the failure to comply with the norms of criminal law, and by "conceptions of criminal responsibility" I mean theories which determine the conditions under which an agent may be held accountable for this failure. I assume that there is a strict connection (that of a necessary and sufficient condition) between the attribution of responsibility and punishability, i.e., an agent can be punished for an act *a* if, and only if, he is (criminally) responsible for it. The conceptions of responsibility are therefore at the same time conceptions of punishability.

Since criminal law is, of all the branches of law, the one most closely related to morality, each of the conceptions of criminal responsibility discussed below could also be defended as a conception of moral responsibility (with due allowances for the obvious and philosophically unimportant differences, for instance the type of norms for the violation of which one is responsible: moral or social norms in the case of moral responsibility and norms of criminal law in the case of criminal responsibility). In fact, some of these conceptions were initially proposed as conceptions of moral responsibility. It also seems that a conception of criminal responsibility in a given legal system is usually a reflection of a conception of moral responsibility presupposed in the morality of the society in which the legal system is intended to function (this sociological claim, however, has no consequences whatsoever for my further analyses).

I assume that each at least *prima facie* plausible conception of criminal responsibility must have the following two features: It must provide that a person *P* can be held criminally responsible for committing an act *a* only if *P* did *a*, and that *a* must be prohibited by the criminal law (let me call these requirements the "basic conditions" of criminal responsibility). Conceptions which fail to satisfy these conditions (e.g., those which *openly* – not just as an unintended and somewhat unlikely consequence of their assumptions – declare that the innocent persons can be held criminally responsible) are omitted in my analysis. The first of these conditions – that for an agent to be responsible for an act he must have at least committed this act – creates the basic link between conceptions of responsibility and the very concept of punishment: One could not speak about punishment but only about social hygiene if this requirement were abolished, and, consequently, if compulsory measures could be used preventively to agents who, owing to their anti-social tendencies, are regarded as very likely to commit criminal offenses.

The *prima facie* plausible conceptions of criminal responsibility differ, however, in how they describe the "state of the mind" in which P must have been at the time of committing *a* if P is to be held responsible for *a*. The most general criterion for distinguishing conceptions of criminal responsibility is whether they assume causal determinism and criminal responsibility to be incompatible (the *incompatibilist conceptions*) or compatible (the *compatibilist conceptions*). Thus, for compatibilist conceptions, the question of the truthfulness of causal determinism is irrelevant, whereas it is crucial for the incompatibilist ones, which imply that if causal determinism holds, then no agent can ever be taken to be responsible for what he did (this combination – incompatibilism *plus* affirmation of causal determinism – is called "hard determinism," in contrast to the combination of "incompatibilism *plus* negation of causal determinism," usually called "libertarianism"). Hard determinism may have different forms, depending on what version of causal determinism is adopted. But in all its forms it provides a justification of why criminals should not be punished but subject to some therapy. In its arguably most popular sociological form, it states that criminals have themselves been wronged – they are the victims of a badly organized society – and thereby should be subject to some kind of therapy rather than punished; punishing them would be unfair as they are not fully or at all responsible for their actions. This view was defended, e.g., by the Sociological School in criminology or by Karl Menninger (2007) and Charles E. Silberman (1978). I shall present this view in more detail in Section 4.

From among the seven conceptions presented below, conceptions 1–3 are incompatibilist, and conceptions 4–7 are compatibilist. I shall present these conceptions by formulating the necessary conditions of criminal responsibility which they formulate; these conditions, together with the previously mentioned "basic conditions" (that a person P can be held criminally responsible for committing an act *a* only if P did *a*, and that *a* was prohibited by the criminal law), constitute necessary and sufficient conditions. An exception should be made for *conception 5*, which, as we shall see, in fact repeats the "basic conditions." The presentation of the conceptions will have a critical character, though a more general evaluation of them, appealing to philosophical anthropology, will be made in Section 5.

2.1 The Incompatibilist Conceptions

An outline of *conceptions 1* and *2* has already been presented in the Introduction. I shall present them now in a more systematic way. I shall not discuss, however, the third conception mentioned in the Introduction, viz. the "cosmic/God's eyes" conception of responsibility, since it will not play any role in my considerations pursued in this chapter, which are devoted to the general justification of the insanity defense. However, this conception will play an important role in my analysis (conducted in Chapters 2 and 3) of the two components (the cognitive and the volitional) of the insanity defense.

According to *conception 1*, P can be held criminally responsible for committing an offense *a* (or any other offense) only if *P* is endowed with free will, i.e., "the ability to do otherwise" (the act *a* and the mental intention to commit *a* must not therefore be causally determined if *P* is to be held responsible for *a*), and free from external coercion (of the so-called *vis compulsiva* or *vis absoluta*). The phrase "any other offense" is justified because, on this conception, free will is treated as a durable power/feature/faculty: If human beings possess this power, they cannot lose it. According to this conception, *P* will be held responsible for action *a* even if this action, though based on free will, was not fully voluntary, i.e., was not free from *both* internal and external coercion. Since this conception implies that free will, if human beings possess it, is possessed *by all human beings* and *exhibited also in their non-voluntary actions* (unless they are caused by *vis absoluta*, in which the decisional component does not appear, or, more controversially, also in *vis compulsiva*, where the decisional component is present), it leads to the conclusion that the criminal responsibility of the mentally sane and the mentally insane should be equalized (should be *none*, if the existence of free will is denied, and should be *full*, if the existence of free will is affirmed). This conception, therefore, determines *by itself* (without the necessity of its supplementation by a conception of mental illness) the model of the criminal responsibility of the mentally insane. This conception is highly counterintuitive because it implies that human beings exhibit free will (assuming that it exists) also in not fully voluntary actions, whereas most of those who believe that free will exists seem to assume (though they seldom make this assumption explicit) that it is only manifested in voluntary actions.

This critical remark leads us to *conception 2*, which says that *P* can be held criminally responsible for committing offense *a* only if *P* is endowed with free will *and* his action *a* was voluntary (free from not only external but also internal coercion). Unlike *conception 1*, which implies that the mentally ill can be held criminally responsible (because internal coercion is not an exculpating circumstance), this conception does not by itself determine the problem of the criminal responsibility of the mentally insane but only in conjunction with a given view of mental illness (specifying whether mental illness is a real entity or a fiction).

It is worth mentioning another incompatibilist conception (I shall call it *conception 3*), which is based on a peculiar understanding of the concept of self-determination. It deserves a closer analysis because if this understanding were the proper one, it would undermine the personalist view of man assumed in this book. This conception was formulated (by Galen Strawson) as a conception of moral responsibility but I shall present it also as a conception of criminal responsibility.[4] It asserts that P can be held morally or criminally responsible for committing an offense a (or any other offense) only if he is *causa sui*, "at least in certain mental respects," such as "preferences, values, ideals, pro-attitudes," which determine the way in which we react to various reasons for action (cf. Strawson 1994: 5–7).[5] Strawson argues, however, that no one can be *causa sui* and thus no one (irrespective of whether he is mentally sane or insane) can be held morally and (if we treat his conception also as a conception of criminal responsibility) criminally responsible (the conception of Strawson therefore, *by itself* – without the need to be supplemented by a conception of mental illness – resolves the problem of the responsibility of the mentally insane). The argument of Strawson is simple (he calls it "the Basic Argument"): An agent always chooses an action in accordance with some previous criteria (or "principles of choice" as he calls them); however, these criteria were either not chosen by him in a "reasoned, conscious, intentional fashion" but imposed on him (by his upbringing, genes, etc), in which case he is not *causa sui*, or they were chosen by him; but if they were chosen by him, they must have been chosen in accordance with some earlier criteria, which means that either he is not *causa sui* (because these earlier – second-order – criteria were in some way imposed on him) or, if these higher-order criteria were chosen by him in light of still higher-order ones, then there occurs *regressus ad infinitum* (an infinite series of the agent's choices), which is impossible. Strawson summarizes his line of argumentation in the following way:

> True self-determination is impossible because it requires an actual completion of an infinite series of principles of choice. So true moral responsibility is impossible, because it requires true self-determination ... We are what we are, and we cannot be thought to have made ourselves *in such a way* that we can be held to be free in our actions *in such a way* that we can be held to be morally responsible for our actions *in such a way* that any punishment or reward for our actions is ultimately just or fair. Punishments and rewards may seem deeply appropriate or intrinsically "fitting" to us in spite of this argument, and many of the various institutions of punishment and reward in human society appear to be practically indispensable in both their legal and non-legal forms. But if one takes the notion of justice that is central to our intel-

---

[4] It should be noted that this was not Strawson's intention, as can be inferred from the quotation invoked further in this text from Strawson's article; Strawson meant it only as a conception of moral responsibility.

[5] Galen Strawson ascribed this conception, rather controversially, to Kant and Sartre, and also (less controversially) to Nietzsche (as noted by Strawson, Nietzsche rejects the very concept of *causa sui*, e.g., in paragraph 21 of his *Jenseits von Gut und Böse*, and in consequence rejects the very concept of responsibility).

lectual and cultural tradition seriously, then the evident consequences of the Basic Argument is that there is a fundamental sense in which no punishment or reward is ever ultimately just (Strawson 1994: 7, 15–16).

Let me pass to an evaluation of this argument. The gist of this argument amounts to the claim that we must be responsible for who we are in order to be responsible for what we do. But this claim rests on two dubious interconnected assumptions: that the very notion of "who we are" is tenable; and that who we are ("our principles of choice") determines our choices. The first assumption seems dubious because arguably one can say only about some people that they have a rigid set of principles (values, preferences, etc.) which determine their choices; most people have a rather fluid set of principles, shaped in the course of the very process of their decision-making. The second assumption seems dubious because there may exist the capacity to decide even against one's own customary "principles of choice" in such a way that the "new principles" of choice are not *presupposed* but *discovered* or *created* – the capacity is (free) will. Thus, even if it were true that we are not responsible for what we are, it would not entail that we act as we do because of who we are: We could still be ultimately responsible for our acts because they are not fully determined by who we are – our capacity of free will underlies this responsibility. Strawson does not consider these objections. But he deals with the objection (similar to the first of these two above) that there may exist "Self" which is independent of character or motives. He points out that such a Self would have to decide "as it decides because of the way it is. And this returns us to where we started. To be a source of true or ultimate responsibility, Self must be responsible for being the way it is. But this is impossible" (Strawson 1994: 20–21). This counter-objection of Strawson, however, can be criticized on the same two grounds indicated above: The Self need not be identical with a rigid set of principles, and the Self may discover or create principles in the course of making a choice. This kind of Self, which is not *causa sui* in the strong – Strawsonian – sense, is nonetheless *causa sui* (in the weaker sense) insofar as it is endowed with free will and thus can always distance itself from the values or principles it accepted in the past (assuming that it did). In other words, Strawson seems to make an (implausible) assumption that in order to be *causa sui*, one must determine, so to say, the totality of one's psychological outfit: emotions, preferences, dispositions, principles of choice etc. Yet the capacity to distance oneself from them seems to be sufficient for holding the Self responsible for his actions. In general, it is hard to agree with Strawson that "however self-consciously aware we are, as we deliberate and reason, every act and operation of our mind happens as it does as a result of features for which are ultimately in no way responsible" (1994: 22). The plausibility of the weaker understanding of *causa sui* is sufficient to profess the personalist picture of human beings.

2.2 The Compatibilist Conceptions

The conceptions discussed in this section assume that criminal responsibility is possible even in a fully deterministic universe.

Conception 4, one defended by many thinkers, to mention only Aristotle (1947), David Hume (1998), or Kazimierz Twardowski (1983), implies that P can be held criminally responsible for committing an offense *a* only if his action *a* was voluntary (free from internal and external coercion). It might be (rightly) objected, however, that my description of this conception is too sketchy as it does not explain satisfactorily why its adherents could assert that an agent who is not endowed with free will but is "merely" free from internal and external coercion can nevertheless be held criminally responsible for his (criminal) acts. One must therefore demonstrate that the lack of coercion allows some other grounds of criminal responsibility (other than free will, which, on this conception, is, *ex hypothesi*, non-existent) to manifest itself. These grounds may be called generally "an agent's individuality." This concept was interpreted in various (although not mutually exclusive) ways by various philosophers: as an agent's character, as an agent's "essence,"[6] as his "decisional centre," as his capacity for self-control, as a set of his *own* beliefs and desires, or as the capacity to respond to moral reasons for and against certain actions (i.e., as being endowed with a reasons-responsive mechanism).

---

[6] Aristotle's term *hekousion*, usually translated as "voluntary," literally means "flowing from the substance," "flowing from the essence" (the substance – *ousia* – is the agent himself); this translation shows immediately why one could argue that an agent can be held responsible for an act done non-coercively: this is his *own* act, *flowing from him* as a separate entity/agent (substance), *not accidental* in relation to his own desires and intentions. Aristotle's definition of voluntary acts is concordant with this etymology: "that of which the moving principle (*arche*) is in the agent himself, he being aware of the particular circumstance" (Aristotle 1947: 1111a23–34). It also follows from this definition that an act may become involuntary in two ways: if it is due to compulsion/coercion (in which case it is *against* the agent's will) or if it is due to unawareness of specific circumstances of a given situation (in which case it is *independent* of the agent's will). But Aristotle would arguably deny that being capable of making voluntary acts is a *sufficient* condition of moral responsibility, for also animals and children can have this capacity; it seems that, in his view, an additional condition needs to be fulfilled, viz. having the capacity (so-called *prohairesis*) to make decisions based on a rational reflection. It is worth adding that Aristotle distinguishes also (in Book III, 1 of *Nicomachean Ethics*) a third category of actions – *ouk hekousia* – which can be translated as "non-voluntary" and which may correspond to various automatic bodily movements which cannot be called "actions."

Depending on how this "ground" is explained, one obtains different variants of this conception. Let me make a short remark on the last variant (based on the mechanism of reason-responsiveness). John Martin Fischer and Mark Ravizza (1998) – its adherents[7] – argue that the mechanism consists of two capacities: regular receptivity – the capacity to recognize moral reasons for or against certain actions – and at least weak reactivity – the capacity to translate these reasons into actions. But, as was argued in the Introduction, reason-responsiveness seems to imply free will. So, in my view, this variant of *conception 4* collapses into an incompatibilist one.

Conception 5, defended, e.g., by Barbara Wootton (1963), states that P can be held criminally responsible for committing an offense a only if his action caused a (or is identical with a); the state of mind of P at the time of committing a (or at any other time) is irrelevant for ascribing him responsibility for a. Thus, only *actus reus*, not *mens rea*, should be taken into account in ascriptions of criminal responsibility: The prosecution neither has to prove intent or recklessness nor query whether the defendant was mentally sane. According to this conception, all crimes become ones of strict liability. Clearly, this conception *by itself* implies that both the mentally sane and mentally insane can be held criminally responsible. Evidence regarding mental condition of the agent, including even the evidence concerning his *mens rea*, should be considered only after the trial process; the trial itself should only be focused on the question of whether the accused "physically" committed the criminal act. It is the experts who, after the trial, should take into account these mental conditions and decide how the perpetrator should be punished. Needless to say, this conception is extremely controversial as it rejects a fundamental assumption of modern criminal law, viz. that the "subjective" side of a crime is equally important as its objective side (the outward act). One can understand, however, why it might have been proposed; Herbert Fingarette contented that "this radical surgery" (as he calls Wootton's conception) was a

> reaction to this miasma of *ad hoc* legal doctrine and evidentiary confusion …: remove the entire issue of mental disability from the trial process, and leave it to the post-verdict assessment and dispositional decisions by experts; let the behavior, not the mental state or condition of the actor, be at issue in the trial (1976: 242).

But, as Fingarette argued,

> such reforms, whatever their procedural efficiencies or inefficiencies, infringe in fundamental ways on the principle that the defendant should have the right to present at his trial a complete defense to an accusation of criminal guilt. Absence

---

[7] This conception is also assumed, e.g., by Stephen J. Morse (2002, 2008b).

of *mens rea* – whether "specific" or "general" – is a defense that is fundamental in common law (1976: 242).[8]

According to *conception 6*, *P* can be held criminally responsible for committing an offense *a* only if the penalty brought upon him is likely to cause a desired change in his behavior. Thus, as Andrew Eshleman put it, calling this conception "consequentialist," the agent can be held responsible only if he "exercised a form of control that could be influenced through outward expression of praise and blame in order to promote or curb certain behaviours" (Eshleman 2016). It is worth noticing that *conception 6* will lead to more frequent ascriptions of responsibility than *conception 4* since the group of people whose actions can be influenced by a penalty will arguably be broader than the group of people whose actions were voluntary, and it will lead to less frequent ascriptions of responsibility than *conception 5* (with its modest requirement of only *actus reus*). Conceptions *5* and *6* are similar in that they do not treat *mens rea* as a condition of criminal responsibility but *conception 6* provides a higher threshold for responsibility ascriptions because, apart from the requirement of *actus reus*, it also demands that the agent be responsive to sanctions. *Conception 6* was also defended by Barbara Wootton (1963), especially in the context of her analysis of the function of punishment (which is in her view purely preventive). Alf Ross, the Danish legal philosopher, summarized Wootton's view of criminal responsibility in the following way (the quotation seems to merge both conceptions – *5* and *6* – but it is justified in the sense that he focuses on the element which is common for both of them, viz. the rejection of the criterion of mental responsibility):

> [T]he criterion of mental responsibility (imputability) should simply be dispensed with as a condition for conviction, and the criminological reaction to crime should be arrived at in each individual case without regard to guilt and only with a view to what in the particular instance will offer the best chance of preventing recidivism. The traditional system, which bases punishment on retribution for guilt, should be replaced, according to this view, by a system designed as a means of preventive hygiene …. Wootton's doctrine amounts to no less than the view that questions of both imputation and imputability be discounted as conditions for convicting a person of an offence, while at the same time they are to be taken into account as

---

[8] This is the reason why Fingarette endorsed a traditional account of the insanity defense – he called it the Disability of Mind defense – which "isolates all the elements essential in assessing culpability and places them in the trial; only questions not essential to the issue of culpability are postponed for expert appraisal after the verdict. Thus optimal efficiency within the limits of justice is achievable" (1976: 243).

circumstances which partially determine the nature of legal reaction to be applied in particular case (Ross 1975: 73).[9]

Ross aptly remarked that if we accept Wootton's view, then the distinction between penalty as a just retribution and preventive measures becomes blurred.[10] A similar observation was made by Herbert L.A. Hart:

> Lady Wootton argues that if the aim of the criminal law is to be the prevention of "socially damaging actions," not retribution for past wickedness, the conventional doctrine puts *mens rea* "into the wrong place." *Mens rea* is on her view relevant only *after* conviction as a guide to what measures should be taken to prevent a recurrence of the forbidden act. She considers it "illogical" if the aim of the criminal law is prevention to make *mens rea* part of the definition of a crime and a necessary condition of the offender's liability to compulsory measures (Hart 2008: 194; quotations from Wootton 1963: 51–52).

Conception 7, defended, e.g., by Hart (2008), assumes that *mens rea* and *actus reus* of an agent *P* are sufficient (jointly with the "basic condition," embracing in fact *actus reus*) for holding him criminally responsible even if his (criminal) act was not voluntary (in the sense of freedom both from external and internal coercion). In other words, *mens rea* is preserved as a condition of criminal responsibility but it no longer embraces the requirement of mental normality (sanity): The question of whether the perpetrator is mentally insane should be transferred to the post-trail phase, in which the main role is to be played by medical experts. In fact, Hart treated his own conception as a "less extreme,"

---

[9] In Ross's terminology, imputation is related to the question of the form of the agent's mental attitude to his act (whether the act was negligent or intentional), whereas imputability concerns the question of mental responsibility/culpability, viz. whether the act can be "imputed" to him.

[10] *Conceptions 5* and *6* also seem to justify, e.g., the punishing of children since their conduct can assuredly be modified by sanctions. It would seem that some of their adherents (especially those with collectivist predilections, advocating the priority of the community over the individual) are inclined to accept this and other morally dubious consequences. This can be seen, for instance, in the way in which *conception 6* was defended by the philosopher Francis Herbert Bradley. In an article advocating eugenics he wrote that the "Chief Good" was "the welfare of the community realized in its members" (1894: 269–270). And, in the same spirit, he argued that punishment should be separated from considerations of guilt and justice, the latter being "but a subordinate and inferior principle. It can hear no appeal from the tribunal of the common welfare" (1894: 276). He added that "once admit that life in this world is an end in itself, and the pure Christian doctrine is at once uprooted. For, measured by that end and standard, individuals have unequal worth, and the value of each individual is but relative, and in no case infinite" (1894: 277); "over its members the right of the moral organism is absolute" (1894: 278).

"moderate" form of the "new doctrine," i.e., of the conception (of strict liability) proposed by Wootton (*conception 5*). He described his own theory as replacing

> not the whole doctrine of *mens rea*, but only that part of it which concerns the legal responsibility of the mentally abnormal. In this more moderate form of the theory a mentally normal person would still escape conviction if he acted unintentionally or without some other requisite mental element forming part of the definition of the crime charged. The innovation would be that no form of insanity or mental abnormality would bar a conviction, and this would no longer be investigated before conviction. It would be something to be investigated only after conviction to determine what measures of punishment or treatment would be most efficacious in the particular case (2008: 195–196).

And in a similar vein:

> [U]nder this scheme *mens rea* would continue to be a necessary condition of liability to be investigated and settled before conviction except so far as it relates to mental abnormality. The innovation would be that an accused person would no longer be able to adduce any form of mental abnormality as a bar to conviction. The question of his mental abnormality would under this scheme be investigated only after conviction and would be primarily concerned with his present rather than his past mental state. His past mental state at the time of his crime would only be relevant so far as it provided ancillary evidence of the nature of his abnormality and indicated the appropriate treatment (2008: 205).

Why was Hart reluctant to endorse an "extreme" form of this doctrine (i.e., *conception 5* – a conception of strict liability)? He discussed his three "misgivings" about it.[11]

First, he asserted that "in a system in which proof of *mens rea* is no longer a necessary condition for conviction, the occasions for official interference with our lives and for compulsion will be vastly increased" (Hart 2008: 206). We might also be punished, e.g., for accidental harm.

Secondly, Hart objected to treating "what we now call punishment (imprisonment and the like) and compulsory medical treatment ... just as alternative forms of social hygiene to be used according to the best estimate of their future effects" (2008: 207). His two objections to "detaching the use of penal

---

[11] Note that Hart interprets Wootton's conception as *eliminating* responsibility; I treat it in a different way – as a (peculiar) conception of responsibility. This difference in terminology, however, does not have any further consequences.

methods" from judgments of responsibility are of a moral and sociological character. The moral objection says that

> if we imprison a man who has broken the law in order to deter him and by his example others, we are using him for the benefit of society, and for many people, including myself, this is a step which requires to be justified by (*inter alia*) the demonstration that the person so treated could have helped doing what he did (2008: 207).

The sociological objection concerns two aspects of punishment which distinguish it from medical treatment and which are likely to be preserved (especially the second one) even if prisons were replaced with "places of safety" (Wootton's term). The first one is that "unlike medical treatment, we use deterrent punishment to deter not only the individual punished but others by the example of his punishment and the severity of the sentence may be adjusted accordingly" (Hart 2008: 207). The second aspect is that "unlike a medical inspection followed by detention in hospital, conviction by a court followed by a sentence of imprisonment is a public act expressing the odium, if not the hostility, of society for those who break the law" (2008: 207). Should these two aspects of punishment remain, then arguably only those can be punished who could have acted otherwise that they did.

Thirdly, against Wootton's argument that reference to *mens rea* should not be introduced into the definition of an offense, Hart argued that "there are some socially harmful activities which are now and should always be treated as criminal offences which can only be identified by reference to intention or some other mental element. Consider the idea of an attempt to commit a crime" (Hart 2008: 208).

Hart summarized his argumentation in the following way:

> I do not consider my misgivings on these three points as necessarily insuperable objections to the programme of eliminating responsibility. For the first of them rests on a judgment of the value of individual liberty as compared with an increase in social security from harmful activities, and with this comparative judgment others may disagree. The second misgiving in part involves a belief about the dependence of the efficacy of the criminal law on the publicity and odium at present attached to conviction and sentence and on deterrence by example; psychological and sociological researches may one day show that this belief is false. The third objection may perhaps be surmounted by some ingenuity or compromise since there are many important offences to which it does not apply. Nonetheless I am certain that the questions I have raised should worry advocates of the elimination of responsibility more than they do; and until they have been satisfactorily answered I do not think we should move the whole way into this part of the Brave New World (2008: 207).

However, Hart's own conception is by no means uncontroversial. Herbert Fingarette, for instance, convincingly argued that this conception exhibits much similarity to that of Wootton (of strict liability), as it contravenes "the principle that the defendant should have the right to present at his trial a complete defense to an accusation of criminal guilt" (1976: 242); in consequence, it excludes "by fiat, and counter-intuitively, the possibility that a just determination of culpability can crucially depend upon whether the person's mind was abnormal at the time of the act" (Fingarette 1974: 293).[12] Furthermore it should be noted that the connection between *mens rea* and sanity may be so close that their separation may prove to be impossible (arguably, one cannot speak about an agent's intent, premeditation, deliberation, or malice without assuming his sanity).

Some more general remarks are called for at the end of this section. The incompatibilist conceptions are more prone to the risk of eliminating responsibility than the compatibilist ones since they make criminal responsibility contingent on stronger metaphysical assumptions, whose truthfulness is a matter of dispute, viz. assumptions about the existence of free will or about an agent's being *causa sui*. If the metaphysical assumptions of a given conception are rejected, then, on this conception, criminal responsibility proves to be an empty concept: It cannot be ascribed to anyone. For instance, as already mentioned, Galen Strawson claimed that "nothing can be *causa sui*, and in order to be truly morally responsible for one's actions one would have to be *causa sui*, at least in certain crucial mental respects" (Strawson 1994: 21). But if these assumptions are true, they also provide a more solid basis for holding an agent responsible for his actions (i.e., a more solid justification of moral and criminal responsibility). It is also not accidental that they are also usually invoked to justify the retributive theories of punishment. These theories assume that what justifies a punishment is that an agent *deserved* it by committing an offense. But the concept of desert is only tenable if a sufficiently strong account of agency is assumed. The strong account of agency is provided only by the conceptions based on the assumption of the existence of free will; so these conceptions provide the best justification of retributive justice. Furthermore, the retributive theories of punishment are, arguably, the only ones which do not treat the agent as a means to some other end (e.g., special or general deterrence) but as an end in itself; and, as can be plausibly maintained, only the assumption of free will confers on the agent moral dignity which justifies

---

[12] Let me recall that, according to Hart, the question of the defendant's mental abnormality, since it was to be examined only after conviction, could be concerned *only* with his present, not past (from the time of committing an offence) mental state (Hart writes "primarily" rather than "only" but it seems to be an understatement: If it were to be examined *after* conviction, the mental state of the defendant at the time of committing an act would, on Hart's conception, be irrelevant, at least for the question of culpability). This point of Hart's conception is particularly controversial.

this kind of treatment (as a fully responsible, autonomous agent, who can be treated *seriously* by the criminal justice system, i.e., by imposing a punishment on him for what he did just because he did it). One could contend that, on this view, punishment is, in a sense, an end in itself but this would be a misleading way of speaking: Punishment indeed does not serve any future – social or psychological – goals but it serves one basic goal: giving the perpetrator his due as a responsible, autonomous agent.

The compatibilist conceptions do not make any questionable metaphysical assumptions, so they do not create the risk that criminal responsibility will turn out to be an empty concept, but also, arguably, provide a weaker justification of criminal responsibility. It could also be argued that some of those conceptions (5 and 6) should more properly be called "conceptions eliminating responsibility" rather than "conceptions of responsibility." But the latter term seems to me to be the correct one, at least with reference to *conception 5*. For even if we dispense with *mens rea*, we can still speak about, however strongly we may be inclined to reject it, a conception of responsibility. More problematic is *conception 6* because of its forward-looking character. Whether we regard it as a conception of responsibility will depend on our semantic associations with the term "responsibility." Some philosophers may deny the very possibility of treating it as a *solely* future-oriented notion while others may be ready to do precisely that.[13]

3 ACCOUNTS OF MENTAL ILLNESS

Let me now turn to the second dimension of models of the criminal responsibility of the mentally insane, viz. the accounts of mental illness. I distinguish two such accounts which I dub the "affirmative" and the "negationist."

3.1 The Affirmative Account

This account implies that the distinction between mental illness/disorder and mental health is fully legitimate: Its adherents might admit that it may be difficult or impossible to provide a value-neutral conception of mental illness/disorder/health, but will add that it is possible to construct a mixed one combining a value and scientific element. One such conception was proposed by James Wakefield. On his account, mental illness/disorder is an objective phenomenon: It refers to some *real* dysfunction of a mental mechanism. By

---

[13] For instance, Jaap Hage admits as a possible *conception of responsibility* the view which allows us to "hold people responsible because of the attractive consequences this has for the future" (2020: 38).

a "real" dysfunction he means one whose recognition does not depend on specific cultural assumptions of the "observer" but is defined without reference to the "observer," viz. as "the failure of a mental mechanism to perform a natural function for which it was designed by evolution" (Wakefield 1992: 373). The value-neutrality of his account, however, is not complete because, as he notices, not every kind of dysfunction is to be viewed as a disorder. For a dysfunction to be a disorder, it must also be harmful for the agent, and what counts as being harmful depends, at least to some extent, on the norms of the agent's culture. However, the value component is secondary in the sense that it "selects" disorders from the set of dysfunctions determined by the scientific component. Wakefield's final definition of a disorder as a harmful dysfunction is as follows:

> A condition is a disorder if and only if (a) the condition causes some harm or deprivation of benefit to the person as judged by the standards of the person's culture (the value criterion), and (b) the condition results from the inability of some internal mechanism to perform its natural function, wherein a natural function is an effect that is part of the evolutionary explanation of the existence and structure of the mechanism (the explanatory criterion) (Wakefield 1992: 384).

This definition is very plausible, although not entirely uncontroversial. The obvious objection that may be raised against it is that it is not always clear what function a given mechanism is supposed to perform. We may therefore not know whether a mechanism has a dysfunction until we know its evolutionary function, and such knowledge, especially in the case of mental mechanisms, may often be difficult to obtain. One could also formulate a different objection to this account – that it does now allow one to distinguish between a mental disorder and mental illness (it is clear that not every mental disorder, e.g., dyslexia, is a mental illness which has to be cured psychiatrically). Yet it should be added that Wakefield's account does not imply that the concept of mental illness is clear and distinct; it recognizes its vagueness – a number of "borderline" cases, with regard to which it is not clear whether they can be legitimately regarded as mental illnesses or not. For instance, while it is clear that endogenous psychoses, such as schizophrenia, paranoia, or bipolar disorder (manic depression) are mental illnesses, it is less clear whether borderline personality disorder, obsessive-compulsive disorder, psychopathy or pedophilia are such illnesses (the dominant opinion seems to be that they are not). There is no place here to analyze in depth the sources of its vagueness, but it is worth noticing that the uncontroversial cases of mental illnesses seem to be connected with the cognitive defect (being "out of touch with reality," having delusions), whereas controversies tend to arise mainly in connection with the disorders which affect the volitional or affective side.

3.2 The Negationist Account

The negationist account is connected with the so-called "anti-psychiatry" movement, a term coined by one of its proponents – David Cooper – in his book *Psychiatry* and *Anti-Psychiatry* from 1967. There are three different claims characteristic of this trend, although it must be stressed that not all unorthodox psychiatrists, i.e., anti-psychiatrists, have defended all of them.

The first claim, which can be termed the "sociological," is the least controversial: It says that *many of the practices of orthodox psychiatry (as it functioned before the 1960s), i.e., the typical attitudes and methods of treatment of the mentally ill within the psychiatric system (e.g., electroshocks, lobotomy), cannot be morally accepted as they are inhumane, lacking in respect for the patients' dignity and rights, based on violence, oppression, the rigidly hierarchical relation between the patient and the doctor.*[14] In the more radical versions of this claim, the critique of the practice of orthodox psychiatry becomes part of a more general critique of the system of (capitalist) power, the "doctor" being seen as a representative of this power. The postulate flowing from this claim was that the psychiatric system should be radically changed so as to guarantee that the dignity and human rights of the patients become recognized and respected.

The second claim, more important in the context of my considerations, is that *mental illness is a social construct or a myth*: The mentally "ill" are not ill in the strict – and proper – sense of an objective dysfunction (only physical illness is an illness in the strict and proper sense, so the argument goes); they just behave in a way which differs from what society regards as "normal"; to put the etiquette of mental illness on them is an insidious attempt at disciplining them and imposing on them the prevailing social norms. On this account, the concept of mental illness is an instrument of stigmatizing socially undesirable conduct and is thereby intentionally used in bad faith by those in power (although it should be added that anti-psychiatrists sometimes also interpreted this concept in a less "unmasking" way, viz. as an expression of sexual, racial, or social prejudices, which may be cherished, or rather, are usually cherished, in an unconscious way). One should also note that the second claim may take a stronger form: viz. that mental "illness," besides being no illness at all (a weaker form of the claim), is also, or at least may be, a privileged form of cognition, offering an access to some other dimension of

---

[14] This inhumanity of institutional psychiatry was especially strongly emphasized by Erving Goffman in his classical book *Asylums* from 1961, which profoundly influenced the "anti-psychiatric" movement. For instance, the works of the Italian psychiatrist Franco Basaglia (1973) have been much influenced by Goffman's analyses.

reality. The claim that mental illness is a social construct or a myth is, obviously, fully compatible with the first one, or even implies it: If a mental illness is a myth (regardless of whether regarded erroneously as non-myth or deliberately invented to discipline those who deviate from what society regards as normal), one cannot be uncritical towards the practices and perhaps even the very existence of the institutions of orthodox psychiatry (which, on this view, is based on a fundamental mistake). The second claim in its stronger form was defended, for instance, by Michel Foucault, whereas Thomas Szasz, perhaps the most famous representative of "anti-psychiatry," defended its weaker form.[15] A short presentation of their views may be in order here as it will help better understand their reasons for adopting the critical stance on the traditional account of mental illness.

In his classic book *Histoire de la folie à l'âge classique* from 1961 Michel Foucault maintained that the concept of mental illness is simply one of many ways in which the state tries to control its citizens. According to this account, mental illness, unlike physical illness, is not an objective phenomenon: The deficiencies to which it refers are *always* socially constructed, distinguished on the basis of subjective ideas and evaluations of those who ascertain them. There exists a certain standard view of happy/healthy/adaptive life in a given society, and anyone who deviates from this standard is considered to be mentally ill. Thus, there exist no strictly scientific, objective grounds for introducing the concept of mental illness. In Foucault's view, the modern understanding of mental illness – precisely as an *illness* – is a consequence of the reinterpretation of madness that took place in the Enlightenment and 19th century: The voice of madness – the voice of Unreason – was no longer considered legitimate as it had been earlier in the Middle Ages and in the Renaissance, when reason could be unreasonable and unreason could be reasonable.[16] In the Middle

---

[15] Although Szasz preferred to speak about himself as an adherent of "anti-coercion" rather than "anti-psychiatry."

[16] This historical interpretation (but not necessarily its philosophical interpretation) is shared also by many other historians. For instance, George Rosen wrote that in this period (the Middle Ages – especially the waning Middle Ages – and the Renaissance) "madness through its linkage with the revelation of religious truth became a means of achieving knowledge. Madness was a primitive form of revelation, revealing the depths of menace, destruction and evil that lurked beneath the illusory surface of reality. Unreason revealed the unbearable, the things in the world upon which one could not otherwise bear to look" (1968: 155). This passage refers mainly to the Middle Ages, but madness was not totally rejected during the Renaissance either – the mentally ill were still to be considered as "different," not as dangerous. Let me only mention Erasmus of Rotterdam's *Moriae encomium* (*In Praise of Folly*), in which the voice of folly is undoubtedly regarded as deserving to be heard: The folly argues that various forms of irrationality are necessary for the functioning of the world (given the precariousness

Ages, various cities may have wanted to dispense at times with the "mad" by means of the famous *Narrenschiff* (ship of fools) – as depicted most famously by Hieronymus Bosch – which left them in other cities or in rural areas, but, in general, the "mad" were tolerated, treated just as somewhat different. But this voice of Unreason was smothered by reason, which, in Foucault's radical view, is nothing more than the face of power, leading to the disciplining of society, to imposing on people a new social-police order. In the course of this process, the exclusion of the mentally ill from society proceeded in two stages. In the first one, which took place in the Enlightenment, the mentally ill, alongside other socially undesirable groups (e.g., petty criminals, vagrants, beggars, prostitutes, prodigals, the dissolute, libertines, blasphemers), which the emerging, ever stronger modern state wished to separate from the rest of society (as a social burden: as useless to its economy – they were viewed as "idle" – and posing a threat to the social order), were interned in special correctional institutions.[17] The internment – "the Great Confinement," as Foucault calls it – did not have a medical function but rather an administrative, social, and oppressive one, aimed at controlling those who did not work and who violated common social standards. It is not accidental, in Foucault's opinion, that the places of internment were located in the former *leprisoria*: The interned were marginalized and stigmatized just as lepers were in the Middle Ages and during the Renaissance – they were perceived as a threat to the social order. The criterion for internment was the mere deviation from social norms; the tolerance of this kind of deviation – large, when folly was regarded as not fully separable from reason – was greatly diminished, all the more so given that "anti-social" people were believed to be in moral error – to have chosen by themselves their

---

and uncertainty of life, and the unreliability of human beings, it is, in a sense, a folly to conceive a child, to get married, to make friendships, to pursue far-reaching goals, etc.), and that many of those regarded commonly as sane are in fact insane. It is worthy of note that depending on the context, Erasmus uses the word "folly" (*moria/stultitia*) in a positive sense (as leading to ignorance and illusion, veiling the darker sides of human existence and blocking access to unpalatable information, e.g., about one's own wife's infidelities, thereby liberating the human soul from various painful concerns) or in a negative sense (as leading to aggression, wars, desire for gold, parricide, incest, sacrilege, etc.), and in a strict sense – mental illness – or a broad sense – that of irrationality. Furthermore, while one encounters much sympathy with folly and skepticism towards reason in Michel Montaigne, Descartes (writing in the post-Renaissance period) is entirely on the side of reason: he no longer believes that folly can give any valuable insights.

[17] The most (in)famous of them being l'Hôpital de la Pitié-Salpêtrière in Paris, established by an edict of 1656; several years after its opening it became a place of confinement for about 6,000 people, 1 percent of the city's population. The residents of this place were forced to work and produce goods but the attempt to transform it into a factory proved to be a failure.

lifestyles. This was an example, on Foucault's interpretation, of not only physical, but also moral – symbolic – violence directed at excluding from society certain undesirable groups of people. At this stage, the mentally ill were not treated as a separate – *sui generis* – category (which implies that madness was perceived as being rooted in morality, and in effect as being connected with evil – as multiplying the evil contained in a socially undesirable act).[18] The differential treatment of the mentally ill came about at the second stage – in the 19th century, in the aftermath of the abolition (in 1786–1793) of the internment system (which, besides being non-humanitarian, generated higher costs than economic output) and of the reforms initiated by William Tuke and Philippe Pinel, which gave rise to psychiatric hospitals. These reforms are traditionally interpreted as humanitarian in spirit: as liberating the mentally ill from the ignorance and prejudices of previous ages (when the mentally ill were put together with criminals, and were treated as curious animals often put on display for inquisitive spectators, and, additionally, often held morally responsible for their mental state), and therefore as aimed at providing them with therapeutic help. Yet Foucault disagreed. He wanted to demystify the purportedly humanitarian character of these reforms by pointing out that the mentally ill were not only tolerated in the Middle Ages and the Renaissance but also, at least to some extent, appreciated. So these reforms can only be viewed as progress in comparison with the period of Enlightenment (when people with mental illness were not separated from criminals). Furthermore, these reforms were not liberating as they retained the *isolation* of the mentally ill (even though the isolation was at the start of this process non-coercive). More importantly, they had, more or less overtly, an ideological goal: The confinement of socially undesirable people (the mentally ill) was not only (or even not above all) to help them but to protect the bourgeois society and its morality; mental asylums were, therefore, an even more efficient instrument serving the moral uniformization of society. Psychiatric practice is, at least on this view, a form of moral tactic aimed at promoting a very specific – dominant, bourgeois – moral lifestyle and suppressing the other lifestyles under the cover of care for the mentally ill. It should be emphasized that, in Foucault's view, the evolution of social attitude towards the mentally ill was not the result of some series of conscious decisions of a controlling agency; rather, it was

---

[18] Yet, as shown by Foucault, the mentally ill were treated in a different way in the legal context – as a separate category: Mental illness was regarded as an excuse. It seems paradoxical that two such different ways of treating the mentally ill could be upheld at the same time. The treatment adopted by the internment institutions implies that the mentally ill person is responsible for his mental state, that this state flows from his (free) will, while the treatment adopted in courts assumed that the mentally ill cannot be blamed for their mental state.

an unintended (though *ex post* predictable and logical) result of the process of emergence of the modern state with its disciplinary ambitions and of a certain type of morality (bourgeois).[19]

As for Szasz's view of mental illness, it is in some points similar to that of Foucault's yet his perspective is different: less historical and sociological and more scientific and philosophical. In his most famous book, *The Myth of Mental Illness* of 1960, Szasz raised the claim that there are no grounds for the belief that mental illness is a scientific category; it is not, unlike any genuine illness (being a scientific category), a physical lesion, a deviation from the anatomical structure, an "abnormal biological condition," or "abnormal functioning of the body" (1974). Rather than being a scientific category, mental illness is a metaphor or a myth constructed by the psychiatric authorities to support the existing social norms. Thus, in contrast to bodily illnesses, mental "illnesses" are invented, not discovered. This "conspiratorial model of madness", as it is often called, was aptly characterized in the following way (in the context of schizophrenia): "Schizophrenia is a label which some people pin on other people, under certain social circumstances. It is not an illness, like pneumonia. It is a form of alienation which is out of step with the prevailing state of alienation. It is a social fact and political event" (Siegler, Osmond, Mann 1969: 950). In Szasz's view, those who are called "mentally ill" can at best be said to suffer from "problems in living" (1974: xi), i.e., from not being capable of adapting themselves to the norms existing in a society or from encountering difficult moral dilemmas which they find themselves unable to resolve (e.g., reconciling the need for intimacy and the need for solitude);[20]

---

[19] It may be interesting to note that Foucault's interpretation of the "history of madness" was considerably influenced by his reading of the essay "Van Gogh, The Man Suicided by Society" written by the French writer Antonin Artaud. After a nervous breakdown, Artaud spent nine years in a mental hospital, where he was subjected to severe treatment including 60 electroshocks (cf. Kotowicz 1997: 61). In this essay, which was a scathing critique of orthodox psychiatry, Artaud defended the view that mental illness is not only no illness at all; it is also a privileged way of knowing; as he wrote:"a tainted society has invented psychiatry to defend itself against the investigations of certain superior intellects whose faculties of divination would be troublesome" (quoted from Kotowicz 1997: 62).

[20] In Szasz's opinion, another good example of such a problem is hysteria, of which he wrote as follows:
> The typical cases of hysteria cited by Freud ... involved a moral conflict – a conflict about what the young women in question wanted to do with themselves. Did they want to prove that they were good daughters by taking care of their sick fathers? Or did they want to become independent of their parents, by having a family of their own, or in some other way? I believe that it was the tension between these conflicting aspirations that was the crucial issue in these cases. The sexual problem – say, of the daughter's incestuous cravings for her father

accordingly, "psychological interventions are directed at moral, not medical problems (1974: x)" and "while medical diagnoses are the names of genuine diseases, psychiatric diagnoses are stigmatizing labels" (1974: xii), which are "used chiefly "to obscure and explain away problems in personal and social relationships" (1974: 182).[21] Szasz has argued that "mentally ill" patients try to solve this and similar problems by playing various games, e.g., the hypochondriac "takes the role of certain medical patients," whereas the schizophrenic "often takes the role of other, invariably famous, personalities" (1974: 237), and one afflicted with frustration and unhappiness takes the role of a sick person and pretends to suffer from weakness and helplessness. In other words, instead of bravely countering the problems that life inevitably carries with it, they prefer to accept the escapist way of assuming that the problems are not inherent in life itself – that they are in fact a manifestation of a curable mental "illness." The very idea of mental illness is therefore grounded in the false belief that life itself is free from inevitable conflicts, and that the ideal of personal or social happiness can be easily achieved. It should be stressed that, according to Szasz, many mentally ill "patients" may subjectively not experience a "problem in living" – they may not define themselves as ill, but they are so defined by other people – thus the role of a mentally ill patient is imposed on them against their will. All in all, in Szasz's opinion, "patients" should be allowed to choose the way they want to be helped by themselves (if they want to be helped at all): "[C]ustodial psychiatry," as Szasz called it, should replace "institutional – coercive – psychiatry." The state should not be a "therapeutic state," i.e., it should not play any role in solving the problems of the mentally suffering; there should be no place for involuntary, psychiatric hospitalization.[22] Consequently, the insanity defense should also be rejected as it implies that the concept of mental illness is a legitimate one. These postulates of Szasz were additionally motivated by his libertarian political convictions. As men-

---

– was secondary (if that important); it was stimulated, perhaps, by the interpersonal situation in which the one had to attend to the other's body. Moreover, it was probably easier to admit the sexual problem to consciousness and to worry about it than to raise the ethical problem indicated. In the final analysis, the latter is a vastly difficult problem in living. It cannot be "solved" by any particular maneuver but requires rather decision making about basic goals, and, having made the decisions, dedicated efforts to attain them (1974: 247).

[21] A similar view of mental illness was defended by Thomas Scheff, who claimed that mental illness is a cultural construct, a medicalization of norm violations, a "residual deviance" embracing those norm violations "for which the culture provides no explicit label" (1984: 31).

[22] As he put it, "We are going towards what I have called a therapeutic state, where we are steadily making society less and less safe for innocent people and are locking up people under medical auspices who are not sick" (Szasz and others 1996).

tioned, Szasz did not maintain that mentally ill people do not need any help; but he believed it should not be the kind of help offered to them in traditional mental hospitals. The "libertarian" reason for this claim is that they undergo in these hospitals an involuntary therapy for an indefinite time; such a form of containment (the so-called "civil commitment") is, in his view, a flagrant violation of individual liberty, and, additionally, further proof of the claim that mental illness is not like any other illness (the mental patient may not leave the hospital as he wishes, whereas generally the medical patient may do so; only in extremely rare cases – such as contagious disease – is the involuntary hospitalization of non-mental patients allowed; cf. Szasz 1963; 1990). Szasz even went so far as to call involuntary psychiatric interventions "crimes against humanity" (1974: 267)," "incarceration in the name of diagnosis" (Szasz and others 1996).[23] As we can see, Szasz's concern with the individual liberty of psychiatric patients underlies another objection to the insanity defense, viz. the objection that it allows indeterminate containment with respect to people who have committed a crime – the containment which, as he maintained, is, precisely because of its indeterminate character, an even more flagrant violation of individual liberty than jail, a more harsh "punishment" (in the common, not legal sense).[24] Szasz aptly remarked that the insanity defense, which may lead to people being detained for an indefinite time, and civil commitment are "like Siamese twins: you cannot abolish one without killing the other" (Szasz and others 1996). Indeed, the alternative we are faced with has been outlined by Szasz in a clear manner: We must choose between, on the one hand, civil commitment for the mentally ill who did not commit a crime *plus* no incarceration (but detainment for an indefinite time) for those of them who committed a crime,[25] and, on the other, no civil commitment for the mentally ill who

---

[23] To Szasz's further dismay, the decisions about the containment of the mental patients were made by the medical profession.

[24] In response to the objection that the abolition of the insanity defense means that if the mentally ill commit a crime, they will go to jail, Szasz said that it is better for them because jails are less cruel than involuntary hospitalization.

[25] Szasz described this first option in a more dramatic way – as involving "imprisonment without trial (involuntary psychiatric hospitalization) and punishment without having been sentenced (psychiatric treatment)" (1990: 560), "imprisoning the innocent and exculpating the guilty" (1980: 120). He also wrote in a more ironic tone:
> On Mondays, Wednesday, and Fridays, the psychiatric prevaricators thus go to court to exonerate the guilty: That is called "psychiatric defense." On Tuesdays, Thursdays, and Saturdays, the same prevaricators go to court to incriminate the innocent: That is called "civil commitment." The lawmakers, the judges, and the attorneys (for both sides) all shamelessly uses these fakes – which is why each of them is as reluctant to expose and demolish the psychiatric defense of the guilty as he is to expose and demolish the psychiatric incrimination of the innocent (1980: 120).

did not commit a crime *plus* incarceration for those of them who committed a crime. If we assume any of the two claims endorsed by Szasz – that mental illness is a myth or that liberty is the supreme value – we must choose the first option.

Allow me to note that the second – libertarian – objection raised by Szasz against the insanity defense may take a stronger or weaker form, something which Szasz did not distinguish quite clearly. In its weaker form, it says that the insanity defense, even if invoked *bona fide*, has pernicious consequences as it justifies a flagrant violation of individual freedom. In its stronger form, it says that the insanity defense is prone to be invoked also *mala fide* – as a pretext to justify holding for an indeterminate time in confinement the defendant whom prosecutors and judges know to have no mental illness at all.[26] Szasz was arguably endorsing mainly its weaker form, although it seems he also occasionally manifested some sympathies with the stronger one.[27]

In summary, Szasz put forward two independent but compatible arguments for the rejection of the insanity defense. He claimed that since insanity (mental illness) is a myth, the institution of the insanity defense is groundless: It relies on a non-existent entity. Yet it seems that he attached more weight to the second – "libertarian" – argument, viz. that the insanity defense is a violation of human dignity as it is inextricably connected with the institution of civil commitment (this argument, to be quite strict, is not just compatible with the first one – that mental illness is a myth – but is also strengthened by it). One can also imagine another argument against the insanity defense which does not play an important role in Szasz's critique, viz. that even if the perpetrator of a crime is insane, he still preserves free will, and thereby can be held respon-

---

[26] The stronger form was defended by, e.g., Joseph Goldstein and Jay Katz, who explicitly wrote that "the insanity defense is not a defense, it is a device for triggering indeterminate restraint" (1963: 868). As they pointed out, if insanity were treated only as "evidence which precludes establishing a crime by leaving in doubt some material element of an offense" (1963: 854), that is, *mens rea*, then the perpetrator would have to be released (since there would be no crime at all, and so no defense would be needed); but if insanity is an excuse, then the perpetrator is deemed not guilty by reason of insanity, and as a result can be detained for an indeterminate time.

[27] This ambiguity in his views on this issue can be discerned, e.g., in the following statement: "The introduction of psychiatric considerations into the administration of the criminal law – for, example, the insanity plea and verdict, diagnoses of mental incompetence to stand trial, and so forth – corrupt the law and victimize the subject on whose behalf they are ostensibly employed" (1974: 267).

sible for his act.[28] We shall return to this argument (which can also be called "libertarian"[29]) in Section 4 of the present chapter.

One point bears stressing: Szasz did not share the political leftist sympathies of many representatives of "anti-psychiatry." In the article "Anti-Psychiatry: The Paradigm of Plundered Mind," which Szasz wrote in 1976 for *The New Review*, we can read: "the anti-psychiatrists are all self-declared socialists, communists, or at least anti-capitalists and collectivists. As the communists seek to raise the poor above the rich, so the anti-psychiatrists seek to raise the 'insane' above the 'sane'" (quoted from Kotowicz 1997: 92). In this article he claimed that the left appeal to the youth who "have nothing to live for, are envious of all those who do, and want to destroy the institutions that give meaning to the lives of 'normal' people" (quoted from Kotowicz: 1997: 93). He believed that "the simplest of human truths is that life is an arduous and tragic struggle" (quoted from Kotowicz 1997: 96), with the consequence, as Zbigniew Kotowicz put it, that "the rewards go to those who are competent, patient, modest, silent, and who accept suffering" (1997: 95); Kotowicz commented on this in the following way:

> With this in mind Szasz's campaign to abolish mental hospitals cannot be put in the same bracket as other protests against the inhumanity of the psychiatric system. He

---

[28] Even though it only appears marginally in his analyses, it takes (when it appears) a suggestive form:
> Today, the role of the physician as curer of the soul is uncontested. There are no more bad people in the world, there are only mentally ill people. The "insanity defense" annuls misbehavior, the sin of yielding to temptation, and tragedy. Lady Macbeth is human not because she is, like all of us a "fallen being"; she is human because she is a mentally ill patient who, like humans, is inherently "healthy"/ good unless mental illness makes her "sick"/ill-behaved (2011: 180).

He also wrote in a different paper that his observation
> that the two paradigmatic practices of psychiatry – involuntary mental hospitalization or civil commitment and the insanity defense or the exculpation of persons guilty of crimes as not guilty by reason of insanity – rests on a philosophically indefensible and morally odious proposition, namely, that unlike the behavior of the sane person, which is governed by free will, the behavior of the insane person is governed by impulses which the subject finds irresistible and for which he or she is, therefore, not responsible (1990: 558–559).

Let us note that this is a very extreme version of the free will doctrine, similar to the one implied by *conception 1* of criminal responsibility (though justified in Szasz's case by his belief that mental illness is a non-existent entity). This conception, as mentioned in the Introduction, is justified by the libertarian but not the personalist picture of man.

[29] As is well known, the term "libertarian" has two quite different meanings; in political philosophy it refers to those conceptions which stress the priority of the value of individual liberty over other values, whereas in the philosophy of mind it is used to describe those conceptions which affirm the existence of free will.

is anti-establishment but in the name of the higher law – the law of the market. And so Szasz would want to eliminate all forms of collective response to mental illness. And there is nothing particularly new in this. As long ago as 1961, Enoch Powell, the then Minister of Health, envisaged closing all mental hospitals and setting up a community care system. This has remained the policy of the Conservative Party, although it is becoming manifest that the notion of "community care" is no more than lip service. It is one thing to shut down hospitals and another to genuinely tackle the society's response to mental illness. This is the difference between the right-wing laissez-faire cost-saving programmes and the Italian experiment, for example (1997: 96).

Finishing my discussion of the second claim of anti-psychiatry (that there is no such thing as mental illness), let me devote a few words to pointing out a paradoxical similarity of this claim with a more popular and more widely accepted claim that the concept of mental illness constitutes a continuum. The continuum view (which arose under the influence of psychoanalysis) amounted to the rejection of the 19th-century account of mental illness as a brain disorder, which some people have and others do not. It resulted in the proliferation of mental illnesses (Attention deficit hyperactivity disorder (ADHD), non-severe depression, adjustment disorders, problems with self-esteem, anxiety, hysteria, and many others), which is visible in the successive editions of the *Diagnostic and Statistical Manual of Mental Disorders*. The paradoxical similarity between both claims (that nobody is mentally ill or disordered, and that almost anyone can be regarded as mentally ill or disordered) lies in the fact that in both cases the very concept of mental illness loses its distinguishing and classificatory function: The first claim implies that no one can be regarded as mentally ill, whereas the second one, at least in its extreme version, implies that everyone can be regarded as – more or less seriously – mentally ill. As can be easily noticed, the second claim can also be used in the critique of the insanity defense – as leading to possible abuses, or to including all criminals in the category of the "mentally insane" (I shall return to this line of critique later in Section 5 of this chapter).

Let me now pass to a discussion of the third claim that appears within anti-psychiatry – *that the mentally ill are entirely or to a large extent responsible for their illness*.[30] It was not that widespread among anti-psychiatrists for the simple reason that it remains in tension with the second – principal – claim. The third claim says that mental illness is a reality, not a myth, and the mentally ill are responsible for their illness. The previous (second) claim does not exclude that the mentally "ill" may be responsible for their "illness" but

---

[30] Patricia E. Erickson and Steven K. Erickson (2008: 14–17) call such a conception of mental illness (which views it simply a failure of personal responsibility) "moral/punitive."

this (possible) ascription of responsibility loses moral weight insofar as mental illness is assumed to be a myth – no illness at all. It is worthy of note that each of these claims implies that mental illness cannot be an exculpatory circumstance in criminal law. In discussing the third claim at greater length, I shall focus on Ronald D. Laing's most famous book *The Divided Self* (from 1960), though this idea can be found also in the works of other anti-psychiatrists, for instance Szasz, who called bodily diseases "happenings" and mental illnesses "actions" ("mental illness is not something a person has, but something he does or is" (Szasz 1974: 167)), thereby suggesting that they are caused by the "ill" agent himself (cf. Szasz 1974: 154).[31]

Arguably, Laing's account of mental illness can be interpreted as implying that mental illness is a genuine defect, but one which has been caused by the mentally ill person himself, so that one can speak about his responsibility for his illness. This interpretation can be justified (though not, as we shall see, unequivocally) by two strands in his argumentation.

First, Laing asserted that there is no unbridgeable abyss between sanity and madness: In his view, schizophrenia (on which he was focused) is in fact a development of certain traits already present in the (sane) personality of a schizoid agent, who suffers from "ontological insecurity" which can take three forms: fear of engulfment (of other people as threatening his autonomy), of implosion (of the world "as liable to crash in and obliterate all identity" (1969: 45)), or of petrification (of depersonalization). A person suffering from ontological insecurity has a diminished feeling of himself as a person who is real, autonomous, "spatially co-extensive with his body," and identical over time. He experiences the division between, on the one hand, his "un-embodied self," and on the other, the world, his own body, and the "false-self systems" associated with the body (which enable him to function in the world but which he does not treat as expressions of his real self). According to Laing, the transition from the schizoid state to schizophrenia proceeds as follows: The division between the "un-embodied," "inner" self and the "rest" (body/false-self systems/the world) becomes ever deeper – the false-self systems become more and more extensive, autonomous, and "harassed by compulsive behavioural fragments" (Laing 1969: 142), and the inner self becomes more

---

[31] Let me recall that, according to Szasz, the mentally ill "play games" in order to (ineffectively) solve their "problems in living." This seems to suggest that he would be inclined to hold them responsible for their "mental illness." But, on the other hand, he argued that the concept of mental illness constitutes a threat to personal responsibility since "for the individual, the notion of mental illness precludes an inquiring attitude toward his conflicts which his 'symptoms' at once conceal and reveal. For a society, it precludes regarding individuals as responsible persons and invites, instead, treating them as irresponsible patients" (1974: 262).

and more volatilized, empty (though self-consciousness is enhanced, accompanied by the feeling of being constantly observed by others), unreal, impoverished, mechanical, and finally dead – fragmented; the fragments of the self start to function independently, without knowing what happens in the others (cf. 1969: 129–144), actions are no longer perceived as expressions of the real self. It means that the unity of personality disappears, the border between the self and the world is obliterated, reflective awareness is no longer possible, and memory becomes chaotic. The transition from being schizoid to being schizophrenic therefore consists not only in the further "dissociation of the self from the body" (1969: 129), but also in the destruction, fragmentation of the self itself. The end result is "chaotic nonentity" (1969: 162). Now, in describing the "transition" of the patient from the schizoid to the psychotic state, Laing writes about the individual who is already far on his road to psychosis in that he is "in a world in which, like some nightmare Midas, everything he approaches becomes dead. There are now perhaps only two further possibilities open to him at this stage: 1. He may decide to 'be himself' despite everything, or 2. He may attempt to murder his self" (1969: 147). Up to this point one might think that Laing makes the schizoid responsible for his transition to psychosis even at this late stage. But Laing adds that "[b]oth these projects, if carried through, are likely to result in manifest psychosis" (1969: 147). And subsequently:

> [S]anity, i.e., outwardly "normal" appearance, dress, behavior, motor and verbal (everything observable), was maintained by a false-self system while the "self" had come to be more and more engaged not in a world of its own but in the world as seen by the self. I am quite sure that a good number of "cures" of psychotics consist in the fact that the patient has decided, for one reason or other, once more to *play at being sane* (1969: 148).

As we can see, Laing's account of the transition is not entirely clear: One may interpret it as implying the responsibility of the agent, but this interpretation is by no means uncontroversial. Laing did not say expressly that the schizophrenic patient is responsible for his illness but there seems to be nothing in his account of the transition from the schizoid state to psychosis that would exclude such an interpretation. It is true that he maintained that, at some stage of this transition, there may be no way back to "normality." It does not have to mean, however, that he believed that the schizoid could not have done so earlier, when the cleft between his "inner" self and his "false-self" system was not so deep.

Secondly, in his account of mental illness, Laing looked at illness from an existential, subjective point of view, as a specific way of life, without invoking any biological factors in his description (his account of the etiology of mental illness is therefore psychogenic). Given this perspective, one could plausibly argue that this description implies that this way of life has been chosen or at least was not resolutely opposed by the patient. Thus, Laing's view of mental illness as developed in *The Divided Self* may be interpreted as implying that the mentally ill person is to a large extent responsible for his illness; though it must be admitted that it is not entirely clear whether Laing himself would endorse this interpretation. For even though he assumed the subjective, existential perspective, he did not deny that an illness may have also organic aspects or causes, and that an important part of the etiology of mental illness is played by the parents of the ill (he developed the famous "good-bad-mad" scenario of the development of psychosis, which was to demonstrate that the suppression of the needs of a child may trigger the process of splitting the self into the "inner self" and "false-self" system).

By way of a digression, let me remark that it is also not entirely clear whether and to what extent Laing endorsed the stronger form of the second claim of anti-psychiatry (the claim, let me recall, that mental "illness" is not only no illness at all but also a privileged form of knowing). What is beyond doubt is that his views on mental illness underwent a certain evolution: In his later works he certainly became closer to this claim, although he seems to have only accepted its partial form: that mental illness is a real illness but also a privileged form of cognition. He had already written in *The Divided Self* that "our 'normal' 'adjusted' state is too often the abdication of ecstasy, the betrayal of our true potentialities, that many of us are only too successful in acquiring a false self to adapt to false realities" (Laing 1969: 12). He developed this line of thought in *The Politics of Experience*, suggesting that mental illness may be a way of counteracting the social pressure to conform to an abnormal society, that the mad may be more sane than the normal, that the mad may have an insight into other dimensions – may become "the hierophant of the sacred" (Laing 1967: 109) (though he did not claim that madness *guarantees* this kind of insight or that this is the only way of achieving it). Furthermore, as already mentioned, he did not maintain that mental illness is not an illness; as he wrote, "madness need not be all breakdown. It may also be breakthrough. It is potentially liberation and renewal as well as enslavement and existential death" (1967: 110). Laing's point was therefore that a psychotic breakdown is not only the onset of the disintegration of personality: It may also (but is not guaranteed to) be a way of coming into contact with some other – mystical – reality. Thus, as Zbigniew Kotowicz noted, there is no reason to maintain that Laing was "romanticizing madness" or "encouraging people to go mad as this would enrich their lives" (Kotowicz 1997: 66).[32]

---

[32] Cf. also the following quotation:
At no point did Laing lose sight of the fact that a breakdown is also "enslavement and existential death." So why should these views provoke such a strong

To sum up, three different claims have been made within anti-psychiatry: (1) that the psychiatric institutions developed within the paradigm of the "orthodox psychiatry" deprive mentally ill patients of their dignity, and violate their rights; (2) that mental illness is not illness at all (the weaker form) and, besides being no illness at all, it is a privileged form of cognition (the stronger form); (3) that mental illness is a real illness, but one for which the patient himself is responsible. As we shall also see more closely in the next section (in this section I mentioned only Szasz's ideas about abolishing the insanity defense), all three claims have exerted a strong – both beneficial and negative – influence on the psychiatric and penal systems. Especially, claims (2) and (3), though different, may lead (and have led) to similar conclusions as far as the criminal responsibility of the mentally ill is concerned, viz. to the equalization of the responsibility of the mentally ill and the mentally healthy. Claim (2) implies that their responsibility should be the same because there is no such thing as mental illness (though, since on this claim there is also no such thing as "normality," it may also be invoked to justify the radical postulate of the abolition of all disciplinary institutions, including criminal law). Claim (3) implies that the responsibility should be the same because the mentally ill are themselves responsible for their (real) illness.

4 MODELS OF CRIMINAL RESPONSIBILITY OF THE MENTALLY ILL: A SECOND GLANCE

As already mentioned in section 1, the Standard Model assumes that the distinction between the mentally ill and the mentally sane is sound, and that the mentally sane can be held criminally responsible, whereas the mentally insane cannot. This model is accepted by most contemporary legal systems. For instance, in the Polish penal code the model is expressed by Article 31:[33]

> § 1. Whoever, at the time of the commission of a prohibited act, was incapable of recognizing its significance or controlling his conduct because of a mental disease, mental deficiency or other mental disturbance, shall not commit an offence.
> § 2. If at the time of the commission of an offence the ability to recognize the significance of the act or to control one's conduct was diminished to a significant extent, the court may apply an extraordinary mitigation of the penalty.

---

reaction? In part this was because Laing's views were conflated with those of David Cooper, his collaborator in *Reason and Violence*. All of Cooper's subsequent writing are far more unrestrained than Laing's. ... Cooper really saw the mentally ill as part of the vanguard in the fight against oppression, a position that Laing never adopted" (Kotowicz 1997: 67).

[33] As mentioned, similar regulations are adopted in most other criminal codes.

§ 3. The provisions of § 1 and 2 shall not be applied when the perpetrator has brought himself to a state of insobriety or intoxication, causing the exclusion or reduction of accountability which he has or could have foreseen.

It is clear that this model implies the affirmative account of mental illness. It is less clear which of the conceptions of criminal responsibility are endorsed by those who introduced it or by those who apply it. At any rate, it is compatible with *conceptions 2* and *4*. When we look at the Standard Model (M1) in the historical perspective, we can discern that this model was also justified in a different way, one somewhat puzzling for the modern reader, viz. by pointing out that *furiosus solo furore punitur* – that the author of a criminal act who suffers from mental insanity is already punished by his madness. To be quite strict, this thesis does not justify M1, since it implies, unlike M1, that the mentally insane criminal *deserves* punishment, though the punishment is madness itself. However, in practice, the effects of this approach are the same as those of M1: The mentally insane criminal is not punished within the criminal justice system. Let us note that the sentence *furiosus solo furore punitur* echoes Justinian's *Digesta*. It seems to be based on the belief that mental illness has a supernatural cause. This was a fairly typical belief in antiquity; as noted by George Rosen, "the belief that illness was inflicted by a supernatural power or by an angry deity as a punishment for sin was widespread among the peoples of the ancient world" (1968: 28).

As mentioned at the beginning of this chapter, the *Perverse model* (Mentally sane → Not-responsible, Mentally insane → Responsible) was never adopted in the past. But a related model, in which the mentally sane are responsible, but the mentally insane are *more* responsible (i.e., mental illness is an aggravating circumstance) was adopted in some medieval legal codes (e.g., in the 7th-century Edict of Rothari, the Lombard king). It was justified by a supernatural conception of mental illness as a punishment for sins (cf. Robinson 1996: 51); on this conception, mental illness of a perpetrator of an illegal act was regarded as additional evidence of his guilt. As we can see, the belief in the supernatural character of madness could support two different conceptions of responsibility of the mentally ill.

In *the Negative Equalization Model* neither the mentally sane nor mentally insane can be held criminally responsible. This model must be accepted by hard determinists, i.e., those who assume a conception which deems free will or being *causa sui* to be a condition of criminal responsibility (*conception 1, 2,* or *3*) and deny their (free will's or *causa sui*'s) existence. This justification was endorsed, for instance, by the representatives of the so-called Sociological School in criminology, who assumed a deterministic conception of human behavior, including criminal behavior (they stressed the importance of social causes). The most famous of them, Enrico Ferri, an Italian thinker from the turn of 19th and 20th century, asserted that the notion of a penalty cannot be legitimately applied given the non-existence of free will; the measures taken by the state against the perpetrators of criminal acts only have a pragmatic justification: They serve *difesa sociale* – a self-defense of the society against potentially dangerous individuals. This line of thought leads to the conclusion that criminals have themselves been wronged – they are victims of society – and thereby should be subject to some kind of therapy rather than being punished. This view has been defended in modern times, for instance by Karl Menninger (2007), who famously wrote that "all the crimes committed by all the jailed criminals do not equal in total social damage that of the crimes committed against them" (2007: 33), e.g., by their educators using improper child-rearing practices.[34] He argued that a large number of crimes are committed by those who feel desperate, indignant, frustrated, helpless.[35] To punish such perpetrators rather than to make attempts at their socialization is, according to Menninger, a "crime."[36] Menninger proposed a radical reform of the criminal justice system. Its basic points are the following: Indeterminate sentences should be introduced; "amenability to social control" should replace the concepts of responsibility and culpability; psychiatrists should not be allowed to participate in criminal proceedings since they tend to be instrumentally used – "as a legal weapon" – by lawyers, and the differences in their opinions compromise the psychiatric profession; their opinions – to be expressed only after the resolving of legal issues – should be limited to determining the proper way of resocializing – to finding the proper "penalty" – for the convict.[37] Since

---

[34] Cf. the following quotation: "The violent destructiveness of the criminal is so often a reflection of the cruel and violent way in which he was treated as a child" (Menninger 2007: 252).

[35] The belief in the social causes of crime usually goes hand in hand with a belief in the fundamental goodness of human nature. But with Menninger it is not the case; he rejects the optimistic view of human nature, claiming that we all are potential criminals, that "an instinct for destructiveness" is in all of us (he even goes so far as to claim that this instinct for destructiveness is one of the main reasons for public resistance to humanitarian efforts to reform the criminal justice system). One may query whether this combination of beliefs is consistent.

[36] This kind of "don't blame me – I'm not responsible" attitude was forcefully criticized by Charles J. Sykes (1993): If everything bad we do is the result of "illness" (of our own or of the society), if, in other words, each of us is a victim, then we must dispense with the notion of personal responsibility. This amounts to the medicalization of the concepts of sin and crime. Sykes also argued that mental health professionals are responsible for it.

[37] Menninger (2007: 142) made a distinction between penalties and punishment; the former are humanitarian, the latter, e.g., "long-continued torture" of seclusion, "pain inflicted over years for the sake of inflicting pain," are to be eliminated from the legal system.

Menninger also assumed a peculiar view of mental illness according to which it is a form of "social misadaptation," for which society itself is responsible (cf. 2007: 160), and from which all people suffer, to a greater or lesser degree,[38] he was against the insanity defense; he also shared Szasz's fear (even though his leftist political views were radically different from the libertarian right-wing Szasz) that it can be used to detain people unjustly (though Menninger at the same time supported indeterminate sentences, to which Szasz was strongly opposed).[39]

The *Positive Equalization Model*, assuming that both the mentally sane and mentally insane can be held criminally responsible, can be supported on various grounds. It is implied by *conception 5* (objective/absolute responsibility), *conception 6* (if it is assumed that the mentally insane are responsive to sanctions), or *conception 1* (if it is assumed that free will exists) since, on this conception, even the mentally insane exhibit free will. As we can see, the belief that free will can never be "suspended" may lead to the rejection of the insanity defense.[40] Furthermore, the *Positive Equalization Model* is justified by *conception 7*, *conception 2* in conjunction with the negationist account of

---

[38] His exact words are as follows: "all people have mental illness of different degrees at different times, and ... sometimes some are much worse, or better" (Menninger 1963: 32).

[39] Overall, the differences between Menninger's and Szasz's views were much deeper than the similarities; it should therefore come as no surprise that it was Szasz who formulated perhaps the harshest critique of Menninger's views. Here is an excerpt of it:
> According to Menninger, the punishment even of persons guilty of the most heinous crimes, is, quite literally, a crime – whereas their crime is not a crime. Lest anyone think that Menninger is championing liberty for lawbreakers, let me hasten to add that he is not championing liberty for anyone; instead, he seeks to lump the "criminal" together with the rest of humanity – everyone being a fit subject for indefinite psychiatric incarceration at the whim of the psychiatrist" (1980: 113).

Szasz, who believed in personal responsibility and was a true champion of liberty, could not accept Menninger's position which amounted to the abolition of personal responsibility and punishment, and to the medicalization of law.

[40] It is worth noting that an extreme application of this kind of reasoning can be discerned in the witch trials of modern Europe; as Daniel N. Robinson put it:
> [D]uring the centuries of witch-hunts, trials, and executions, the insanity defense is virtually absent in trials for witchcraft itself. For all the powers that might be attributed to Satan, the Church remained resolute in denying that the devil could rob persons of their free will. Were this otherwise, the very grounds on which eternity is spent in heaven or hell would be removed. Satan's power can extend only as far as God allows, and the line is drawn at man's moral freedom. In this understanding, then, the possessed are not passive victims but willful collaborators (1996: 63).

mental illness and with the acknowledgment of the existence of free will, or *conception 4* in conjunction with the negationist account of mental illness.[41] Practical arguments have also been invoked in favor of this model, e.g., the fear that the insanity defense will be abused, i.e., treated instrumentally as a tool for shielding guilty offenders from criminal responsibility (the fear may be justifiable if the list of various mental illnesses is extended), or the putative fact that "insanity trails are regarded as the modern-day equivalent of Roman circuses in which psychiatrists, our contemporary gladiators, testify at great public expense to absurd propositions that bring both law and psychiatry into disrepute" (Brooks 1985: 126). This model was very rarely implemented in legal systems yet there are some examples. Perhaps the best known would be Idaho,[42] where in 1982 the insanity defense was abolished for the first time in the history of the US. The consideration of insanity was eliminated from a criminal trial, which was to be restricted only to ascertaining *actus reus* and *mens rea* (the regulation was, therefore, similar to the one proposed by Hart).[43]

---

[41] It should be noted that the negationist account undermines the very concept of internal coercion.

[42] Earlier attempts to abolish the insanity defense in the US were made between 1908 and 1928 by three state legislatures (Mississippi, Washington, and Louisiana). For instance, the law abolishing the insanity defense enacted by the Washington legislature in 1909 had the following content:
> It shall be no defense to a person charged with the commission of a crime, that at the time of its commission he was unable, by reason of his insanity, idiocy, or imbecility, to comprehend the nature and quality of the act committed or to understand that it was wrong; or that he was afflicted with a morbid propensity to commit prohibited acts; nor shall any testimony or other proof thereof be admitted in evidence (Washington Criminal Code par. 6, 1909).

Another law – that passed in Mississippi in 1928 – abolished the insanity defense in homicide cases (the defendant, however, could present evidence of his mental state; if the evidence was accepted by the jury, it could find him guilty but insane; in that case, his punishment was life imprisonment rather than – as in the case of mentally sane murderers – death). However, all these laws were struck down by the state supreme courts as unconstitutional (violating the defendant's due process rights).

[43] However, the Idaho law admitted an examination of the defendant before a trial; if he was declared to be lacking competence to stand trial, he would be placed in a mental facility and only tried if he regained his ability to participate in his own defense. This, of course, creates the risk that the defendant's lawyers will try to introduce the insanity defense through the back door; as was noted by one of the prosecuting attorneys quoted by Gilbert Geis and Robert Maier:
> [I]t is probably incorrect to say that Idaho "abolished" the insanity defense. The new tactic of defense attorneys in our jurisdiction is to challenge an individual's ability to aid his attorney in the preparation of his own defense. If successful in that endeavor the defendant may never have to be tried under our statutory scheme. Thus, our "abolition" has shifted the emphasis from asserting the defense during the trail to pre-trial. Although the standards are different, it

The only possible verdicts are guilty and not guilty; if the defendant is declared guilty but there is reason to believe that his mental state is a relevant factor for the determination of his sentence, then the psychiatric examination is to be conducted in order to ascertain the extent of his mental illness, the prognosis for rehabilitation, the availability of treatment and level of required care (since the defendant is *guilty*, all forms of care should, strictly speaking, be viewed as a punishment). The motivation for the enactment of this law was complex:

> Persons in positions of authority in regard to mental health law reform in Idaho had formed a virtual consensus supporting abolition. That consensus was firmly based on a belief that the insanity plea had been blatantly misused and had failed to provide either satisfactory treatment for offender or adequate community protection against them. Combined with this conviction was the popular view, strongly held by residents of this isolated, highly religious state, that all human beings ought to take personal responsibility for their behavior, that they should not be able to avoid punitive consequences of criminal acts by reliance on either a real or a faked plea of insanity (Geis, Meier 1985: 73).[44]

After Idaho, several other states also abolished the insanity defense. The differences between their solutions are not deep: While some of them (Idaho, Montana, Kansas, Utah) have no specific insanity defense and the verdicts they admit are only guilty or not guilty (though Montana, Kansas, and Utah, for example, allow evidence of mental disease or defect for purposes of negating *mens rea*), some others (e.g., Kentucky, Michigan, Alaska, Delaware, Georgia, Illinois, Indiana, New Mexico, South Carolina, South Dakota, Pennsylvania) have some weakened form of this defense because, in addition to the verdict "not guilty by reason of insanity," they admit verdicts of "guilty but mentally ill" (cf. Erickson, Erickson 2008: 102). A defendant who is declared guilty but mentally ill is held responsible for his act: He is punished (as being guilty) and, while serving his sentence in prison, simultaneously given (as mentally ill) medical treatment. This solution clearly shows that "medical insanity" is

---

doesn't appear to be as difficult to have an individual certified not to be able to assist his attorney in preparation of his own defense as it would be to challenge the intent aspect of a particular crime" (1985: 79–80).
Furthermore, in order to determine whether the condition of *mens rea* is satisfied, some analysis of the mental state is necessary; so the abolition of the insanity defense is not full (though, it is substantial, because the prosecuting attorney does not have to prove that the defendant knew at the moment of committing the prohibited act its normative quality, or that he could control his action).

[44] Seeking to determine the causes of this decision, Geis and Maier also highlighted the fact that "Idaho was the first jurisdiction to act in the wake of the mood of public outrage after the acquittal of John W. Hinckley, Jr., on the grounds of insanity, following his attempt on the life of President Reagan" (1985: 73).

something different from legal insanity (a defendant may prove that he was mentally ill at the time of the crime but fail to prove that he was legally insane). The attitude of the US legal system to criminal offenders who are mentally ill deserves, however, a more versatile analysis, one taking into account also a broader, sociological context. I shall present such an analysis in Section 5. I shall finish the following section with a presentation of the Swedish regulation of the criminal responsibility of the mentally ill, which, as we shall see, is similar to the Idaho regulation yet was adopted for different reasons.

Sweden adopted a legal regulation in 1962 according to which if the accused has committed a criminal act in a state of mental insanity the criminal court is obliged to decide that he is *guilty/criminally responsible but mentally insane* (rather than, as in most other countries, those which assumed the Standard Model, that he is not guilty/not criminally responsible by reason of insanity) and, subsequently, may punish him more leniently or not punish him at all but instead place him in mental hospital.[45] As we can read in the Swedish penal code, mental illness cannot release an offender from responsibility – it can only be a mitigating circumstance:

Ch. 29. Section (3) In assessing penal value, the following mitigating circumstances shall be given special consideration in addition to what is prescribed elsewhere, if, in a particular case:
1. the crime was occasioned by the grossly offensive behavior of some other person,
2. the accused, in consequence of a mental disturbance or emotional excitement, or for some other cause, had a markedly diminished capacity to control his actions,
3. the actions of the accused were connected with his manifestly deficient development, experience or capacity for judgment,
4. the crime was occasioned by strong human compassion or
5. the act, without being free from criminal responsibility, was such as is covered by Chapter 24.
The sentence imposed may be less severe than that prescribed for the crime in question if this is called for having regard to the penal value of the crime.

Ch. 30. Section (6) A person who commits a crime under the influence of a serious mental disturbance may not be sentenced to imprisonment. If, in such a case the court also considers that no other sanction should be imposed, the accused shall go free from sanction.

---

[45] Let me recall that a similar solution was proposed (independently of the authors of the Swedish criminal code) by one of the greatest 20th-century legal philosophers, Herbert L.A. Hart (2008). Hart, as already mentioned, opted for transferring the problem of the mental competence of the accused (or, rather, the convict) to the post-trial stage; at the trial stage the judge was to resolve only the issues of *mens rea* (intent, negligence, or recklessness) and *actus reus*. However, his reasons for adopting this solution, which I have described in Section 2.2, were different from those of the Swedish legislators or from those dominant in the case of the Idaho legislation.

Ch. 31. Section (3) If a person who has committed a crime for which the sanction cannot be limited to a fine, suffers from a serious mental disturbance, the court may commit him for forensic psychiatric care if, having regard to his mental condition and personal circumstances, admission to an institution for psychiatric care combined with deprivation of liberty and other coercive measures is called for.
If the crime has been committed under the influence of a serious mental disturbance, the court may decide that a special release inquiry under the Act on Forensic Psychiatric Care (1991:1129) shall be conducted during the time in care if there is risk for relapse into serious criminality of a serious kind by reason of the mental disturbance.
The court may, in conjunction with a committal to forensic psychiatric care impose another sanction, but not imprisonment or committal for other special care, if this is called for having regard to the previous criminality of the accused or for other special reasons.

Thus, the Swedish solution abolishes the insanity defense but separates criminal responsibility from punishability. Mentally insane offenders are not acquitted: If they have committed a crime then they are declared guilty/culpable/criminally responsible. But it does not mean that they are punishable just like mentally sane offenders: Their illness is taken into account at the stage of determining sanctions.. This implies that what is decisive for legal reaction is the mental state of the accused at the time of trial, not at the time of committing an offense. From what has been said so far it follows that the Swedish regulation of criminal responsibility of the mentally insane (just like the regulation from Idaho) does not lead to the full equalization of the legal position of mentally insane and mentally sane offenders.

What reasons stood behind the Swedish regulation? According to the Polish sociologist and journalist Maciej Zaremba (2008), the regulation is a result of an incoherent fusion of two different conceptions of criminal responsibility. On the one hand, it was inspired by the Sociological School of criminology (especially by Enrico Ferri), which, as already mentioned, postulated the abolition of the concept of criminal responsibility on the grounds that since determinism is true, no agent can be deemed guilty, and therefore no punishment is justified (the state can defend against perpetrators of crime but the measures taken by the state cannot be called punishment because they are not the realization of justice but *difesa sociale*). If this conception were realized consistently, the result would be the *Negative Equalization Model*. In fact, Ferri's conception influenced the thought of the Swedish psychiatrist Olof Kinberg, who postulated such a model, eliminating the concepts of guilt and responsibility from criminal law considerations. The state, assisted by psychiatrists, was to isolate the most dangerous individuals, thereby realizing the utilitarian goal of maximizing social utility rather than the goal of retributive justice. This view underlay the project of a penal code (called the "Law of Protection") proposed by the Swedish Minister of Justice Karl Schlyter in 1956: The project did not avail itself of the concept of punishment, but rather that of "consequences"; the consequences could also be imposed for an indefinite length of time; everyone (the mentally insane and the mentally sane) could face criminal proceedings but no one could be declared guilty. However, this radical but consistent project was ultimately rejected.[46] On the other hand, the Swedish solution was influenced by the commonsense, standard view according to which the mentally insane should be treated differently from the mentally sane; on this view, only the latter deserve to be punished. The eventually adopted compromise solution tried to reconcile these two different conceptions: It assumes that both mentally insane and mentally sane criminals are responsible for their acts but the distinction between them can be introduced at the stage of determining the consequences of their actions. This is indeed paradoxical: The theory of Enrico Ferri implied that no one can be criminally responsible, while the Swedish code, even though it was influenced by this theory, implied that all (including the mentally insane) can be criminally responsible. One might think that this solution, as far as its practical consequences are concerned, does not differ from the Standard Model, but the reality is very different: The Swedish solution has had several non-humanitarian consequences (cf. Zaremba 2008). First, the accused who is mentally insane has to take part in the criminal proceedings. Secondly, if an agent committed the crime in a state of mental incompetence but is healthy during the criminal process, then he will be punished (just like the criminal who committed the crime in a state of mental competence). Thirdly, a large number of mentally ill convicts are punished rather than sent to mental hospitals.

---

[46] One should add that the deterministic view of human beings, as well as the blurring of the border between the competences of judges and psychiatrists, which underlay this project, were criticized, e.g., by the Social Democrat politician Georg Branting in his article from 1943 "Legal Corruption, or the Fall of the State of Law in Sweden," and by Professor of Law Ivar Strahl , who was strongly against the rejection of the concept of guilt (cf. Zaremba 2008). One can also speculate that a certain role in advancing this project could have been played by an idea advocated by some legal philosophers from the Scandinavian branch of legal realism (e.g., Alf Ross). This is that "responsibility" is a technical, empty, or functional concept, not carrying any moral weight, and that the notions of "guilt," "culpability," or "punishment" are metaphysical fictions and as such should be dispensed with. It should be stressed, however, that Ross himself was in favor of the Standard Model based on *conception 4* (cf. Ross 1975).

5 THE PROBLEMS OF DEINSTITUTIONALIZATION

The criminologists Patricia E. Erickson and Steven K. Erickson have advocated an interesting two-part thesis:

(1) that there prevails in the US

> a negative public sentiment and policy toward the mentally ill [caused by the fact that mental illness came to be regarded] as a failure of individual responsibility rather than an illness requiring a humane orientation ... [and] reframing mental illness as a failure of individual responsibility, along with a continuation of the traditional criminal law model, created a shift to a punitive stance toward the mentally ill – hence the criminalization of mental illness (Erickson, Erickson 2008: 8–9);

(2) that one of the important causes of this "reframing" of mental illness was the "anti-psychiatric" movement.

As already mentioned, it may seem paradoxical (even though it is by no means illogical) that the "existential" view of mental illness typical for anti-psychiatry could have had non-humanitarian consequences, i.e., could have led to the harsh treatment of the mentally ill, whereas the "biological," "reductionist" account of mental illness is likely to lead to the humanitarian treatment of the mentally ill. Yet the paradox disappears if we recall that the existential view (unlike the biological one) may imply individual responsibility for mental illness; it may lead to the conclusion that the mentally ill are themselves to blame for their predicament, and that thereby mental illness is to be regarded as a moral failure. If, as has happened in the US, the "existential" account is combined with the retributive theory of punishment, the treatment of the mentally ill is likely to be especially harsh. Thus, even though anti-psychiatry was to a large degree a reaction against the non-humanitarian treatment of the mentally ill, perhaps as an unintended side-effect it may itself have led to the decrease in empathy towards the mentally ill. After all, if they are not mentally ill at all or are responsible for their mental illness, then the important grounds for empathy disappear. Yet it is clear that the process which led to the "punitive stance" towards the mentally ill was caused by many factors, including a genuine concern for the well-being of the mentally ill, not only by the view of mental illness (supported to some extent by "anti-psychiatry") as a failure of individual responsibility. A crucial stage of this process seems to have been the "deinstitutionalization of mental illness" – "the policy of moving severely mentally ill people out of large state institutions and then closing part or all of those institutions" (Torrey 1997: 8). This process and its causes will now be described in more detail.

The process began in the 1950s and gained momentum in the 1970s as a result of the critique of "institutions" which, as was already mentioned in Section 3.2., were often indeed brutal, cruel, and dehumanizing. This phenomenon was described suggestively in Ken Kesey's *One Flew over the Cuckoo's Nest* (1962) and Mary Jane Ward's *The Snake Pit* (1946), with patients in mental hospitals given cold baths, lobotomies, and electroshock treatment. Mental hospitals therefore not only fulfilled a therapeutic function, but also, as stressed by Erickson and Erickson (2008: 15), a "containment function." Erickson and Erickson, however, aptly noted that "while the conditions in state mental hospitals rightfully came under attack, the conditions themselves do not explain deinstitutionalization and the movement to community care" (2008: 30). Moral indignation at the conditions prevailing in mental hospitals was therefore the initial cause of the process of the deinstitutionalization of mental illness. But it had to be supplemented by several others for the process to take place.

First, one must stress the role of the cultural revolution of the 1960s (and its "child" – anti-psychiatry), which led to the emphasis of the importance of individual rights, personal autonomy, dignity, anti-paternalism, and the concomitant protest against all – or at least all arbitrary – forms of state coercion. One of its consequences was giving the mentally ill the right to refuse treatment: Involuntary treatment and hospitalization were severely criticized and were only accepted if a mentally ill person could harm himself or other people. As already mentioned, this argument was often raised by representatives of the anti-psychiatry movement, notably by Tomas Szasz, who argued that involuntary hospitalization is crueler than incarceration: The former is for an indeterminate time, the latter determinate.[47]

---

[47] Yet it should be stressed that Szasz cannot be made co-responsible for the deinstitutionalization process. He was equally strongly opposed to involuntary hospitalization and involuntary dehospitalization; he wrote very critically about it and in a deeply humanitarian spirit:

> In the past, thousands of individuals were forcibly incarcerated in mental hospitals, often for life; that was bad enough, but at least many of these unfortunate persons could make the asylum their home. Now the situation is even worse, with thousands of people not only being forcibly incarcerated in mental hospitals, but also forcibly evicted from them as soon as they show any sign of adapting to their new environment. Then the cycle of forcible hospitalization and dehospitalization is repeated over and over again, depriving the "mental patient" of a predictable and stable environment both within and without the insane asylum (1990: 561–562).

Secondly, the process might also have been influenced by the conservative – libertarian but not personalist – conception of human beings, which assumes that they are endowed with free will which can never be "suspended," and which therefore is active even in agents who suffer from mental illness.

Thirdly, a number of medical experts strongly believed in the efficiency of the pharmacological treatment of mental illness (especially antipsychotic drugs from the 1950s, e.g., Chlorpromazine-Thorazine, introduced in 1954, which, within one year from its introduction, had been given to more than 2 million patients), which could be conducted outside mental hospitals. It was also believed that long-term stays in hospitals "produce[d] institutional behavior and a tendency to chronic illness (Erickson, Erickson 2008: 26)" and that thereby deinstitutionalization served autonomy, liberty, and dignity of mentally ill persons.

There was, however, also, a fourth – economic – cause, connected with the fact that hospitals for the mentally ill were expensive. Edwin F. Torrey plausibly argued in his important 1997 book *Out of the Shadows. Confronting America's Mental Illness* that this was the main cause of deinstitutionalization. More specifically, it was the introduction in 1965 of federal welfare programs such as Medicaid and Medicare that accelerated the process. Since the programs did not include state psychiatric hospitals (the states had to pay themselves for their sustenance) the incentive arose for the states to shift the costs and responsibility by closing many of these hospitals and transferring the patients to nursing houses or general hospitals, which were financed by the federal government's welfare programs. One can therefore justifiably maintain that "federal dollars have contributed substantially to disjointed, uncoordinated care of mentally ill individuals" (Torrey 1997: 105).

As a result of these various causes, the "deinstitutionalization of mental illness" took place, which, in Torrey's view, "has been a major contributing factor to the mental illness crisis" (1997: 9). Torrey called deinstitutionalization one of the greatest social experiments in the history of the US: While in 1955 there were about 560,000 patients in mental hospitals (from a population of 164 million), in 1994 there were only 72,000 (of a population of 260 million). The difference, as noted by Torrey (1997: 8–9), will prove to be even higher if we take into account the change in population: If the population in 1955 had been at the same level as in 1994, the number of patients in mental hospitals would have totaled around 885,000. It is also worth emphasizing the fact that the most seriously mentally ill were discharged from hospitals (about

---

His blame may only consist in having contributed (by his works) to creating a climate in which mental illness was no longer regarded as illness.

50–60 percent of those discharged were schizophrenics and about 10–15 percent were manic-depressive or severely depressive patients).

What were the consequences of this "social experiment"? It was believed that the mentally ill would take care of themselves and/or would be taken care of by local communities. Yet this expectation proved to be ungrounded in many cases. The mentally ill who were discharged from hospitals often started to take drugs and abuse alcohol (the result of deinstitutionalization was therefore also detreatmentalization), they frequently refused to participate in pharmacological treatment (because the mentally ill rarely regard themselves as ill), became homeless, and, finally, many of them turned to crime. As a result, there took place what Torrey called the "transinstitutionalization" of the mentally ill from asylums to prisons. Prison proved to be a disastrous alternative to mental hospitals, which is illustrated, for instance, by a high suicide rate among the incarcerated mentally ill (though it should be stressed that transistitutionalization was, of course, an *unintended* side-effect of deinstitutionalziation).[48] Erickson and Erickson aptly noted that "the proponents of deinstitutionalization ... created a climate that was less tolerant of the mentally ill and more willing to use prisons and jails as their places of confinement (2008: 25); and in similar vein: "many of the older commitment laws were predicated on recognizing this difference [between the mentally ill and the mentally healthy], while much of the 1960–70 'liberation' from psychiatry was guided by seeing the mentally ill as the same as everyone else" (2008: 194).

Let me summarize the above description of changes in the situation of the mentally ill: Since the "deinstitutionalization of mental illness" was, in large part, based on unduly optimistic premises (e.g., that the mentally ill can take proper care of themselves), it entangled the mentally ill in criminal behavior, for which they were held responsible, just like the mentally healthy (which was, to some extent at least, a result of the reinterpretation of mental illness as a failure of individual responsibility, and the popularity of the libertarian view of human being); in consequence, "transinstitutionalization" took place.

It is clear that one should not interpret the above analyses one-sidedly – as justifying an overall negative evaluation of the changes in the approach to the mentally ill that took place in the US in the 1960–1970s, and as postulating a return to the state from before the "anti-psychiatry" revolution. The truth,

---

[48] This process jibes with the so-called balloon theory, which says that "prison and psychiatric hospital population are inversely correlated: as one rose the other fell – push in one part of a balloon and another part will bulge" (Torrey 1997: 34). One may ask, however, why the juries so often decide to direct the mentally ill to prisons for a fixed period than to mental hospitals. One of the reasons may be their fear that psychiatrists may discretionally decide to release them, accompanied by the conviction that the mentally ill are themselves to blame for their illness.

of course, is much more complex. One should not underestimate the positive effects of deinstitutionalization (which Torrey called "fundamentally a good idea that was carried too far" (1997: 87)) and anti-psychiatry. To give one of many examples, the *Psychiatria Democratica* movement in Italy, founded by the "anti-psychiatrist" Franco Basaglia, led to the adoption of a law in 1978 (the so-called Basaglia's law) which improved the situation of the mentally ill, protecting their civil rights. One should also remember that "anti-psychiatry" did not engender negative effects by itself but jointly with a number of other causes (e.g., the belief in the efficiency of the pharmacological treatment of the mentally ill), which may have played an even more important role. Finally, it needs to be stressed that deinstitutionalization proved to be beneficial for many, or even the overwhelming majority, of patients; Torrey (1997: 144) admits that 90 percent of mentally ill people were satisfied with this policy, though he adds that a substantial minority found themselves "in terrible conditions" (e.g., in 1994, 150,000 mentally ill people were homeless, and 159,000 incarcerated in jails and prisons (1997: 85)). Accordingly, it is difficult to draw up a balance sheet of the costs and benefits. But the very existence of these negative side-effects fully justifies Torrey's claim that important corrections to the approach to mental illness need to be introduced. He provides a list of very reasonable recommendations.

First, the idea of the involuntary hospitalization of the mentally ill, including those who are not likely to harm themselves or others, should be rehabilitated since the liberal approach to this issue has had unintended and undesirable consequences.

Secondly, Torrey convincingly argues that we should abandon the continuum/spectrum concept of mental illness (which, as I argued earlier, is structurally similar to the claim that there is not mental illness at all). He postulates that the term "mental illness or disorder" should be reserved for really serious problems – functional brain abnormalities or impairments (e.g., schizophrenia, manic depression, autism, severe forms of depression, panic disorder): "It is necessary to return to the 19th century idea that these illnesses are in a different category from problems of mental health" (1999: 199). They should also, according to Torrey, be conceptually merged with brain disorders called the neurological illnesses (e.g., multiple sclerosis, Alzheimer's, Parkinson's). This merger would have two important advantages: It would weaken the stigmatization of the mentally ill (because mental illness would be conceptualized as brain disorder, not as a failure in individual responsibility), and it might also accelerate research on mental illnesses (e.g., neuroscience research on the causes of schizophrenia would be promoted).[49] Accordingly, instead of devoting energy and resources to the people who suffer from minor mental problems that do not deserve to be regarded as mental illnesses or disorders, we should focus our attention on counteracting real or really serious mental illnesses. In Torrey's opinion, too much effort has been spent on so-called mental health problems rather than on mental illnesses. Somewhat surprisingly, anti-psychiatry may to some extent be helpful in this context. The anti-psychiatric view may be used to justify cutting the spectrum and making a division between serious or imaginary (or at best non-serious) mental disorders. The latter would be a myth in Szasz's sense. Clearly, this kind of usage of anti-psychiatry is not quite true to the intentions of its adherents, who were apt to defend the claim that *all* mental illnesses are not true illnesses. To follow this second recommendation would lead to limiting the grounds for raising the insanity defense. It would, e.g., lead to the abolition of the so-called "syndrome defense," which mitigates or abolishes criminal responsibility (examples of syndromes invoked within this defense are premenstrual syndrome or battered wife syndrome); this postulate will be additionally supported by considerations devoted to the critique of the volitional component pursued in Chapter 3.

The third recommendation made by Torrey refers only to the context of the US: There should be single-responsibility funding (rather than funding which provides an incentive to the states to shift the responsibility for the mentally ill to the federal government).

Let me summarize. The influence of the cultural revolution of the 1960s on criminal law was multifaceted. The revolution led to the development of the negationist account of mental illness (as a "myth"), which may have induced politicians to adopt the Positive Equalization Model. Yet such a model has only been explicitly (at the legislative level) accepted in some states. And in those states the reasons for adopting was probably different: Legislatures were arguably more influenced by *conception 1*, with its libertarian (but not personalist) assumption that also the mentally ill are responsible, and by more prag-

---

[49] One can also interpret Torrey's postulate of restricting the concept of mental illness to brain disorders in a philosophical way. The interpretation would imply that one can speak about mental illness only if it leads to the loss of the status of personhood in Max Scheler's sense. According to Scheler (2014), one of the conditions of personhood is having the spiritual center, which can be viewed as a source of human intentional acts. If we explain someone's action in causal (objective terms) terms, and not in terms of his intentions, then we imply that this person's spiritual center is empty. A patient is therefore mentally ill if he lacks this spiritual center. Two other conditions of personhood mentioned by Scheler are the capacity to understand the difference between one's own and others' mental states, and the capacity for controlling one's instinctive impulses. A patient who does not fulfill the first condition is likely to fail to satisfy the remaining two.

matic arguments, e.g., fear that the insanity defense will be abused, leading to exoneration of guilty and deserving agents. The fact that this model was not accepted in many states could have been attributed to some extent to the countervailing idea of this revolution, viz. the idea that criminals themselves have been wronged (that the oppressive "society" is guilty), and that – consequently – the proper reaction to a crime (irrespective of whether committed by the mentally sane or insane) is subjecting criminals to therapy, not putting them in prison, or at least treating them in a humanitarian way. However, strictly speaking, this last idea implies the Negative Equalization Model, according to which both mentally ill and mentally healthy people are supposed to be subject to a therapy rather than punished (this model was never adopted as the official one). Another important aspect of the cultural revolution was a celebration of "transgression," and even though only few people engaged in the revolution rejected the very idea of crime, many postulated that the number of crimes should be limited. This postulate has been to some extent realized (e.g., there took place the depenalization of homosexuality).

6 EVALUATION OF THE MODELS

Even though the main goal of this chapter was to distinguish various models of the criminal responsibility of the mentally ill, and to identify their philosophical underpinnings, one cannot stop here and refrain from at least attempting an evaluation. In point of fact, my presentation of the various models, especially of the models of criminal responsibility, was critical and not purely descriptive. However, the evaluation made so far must be supplemented by some additional remarks.

6.1 Conceptions of Criminal Responsibility

Let me start from the first dimension of the models – various conceptions of criminal responsibility. I have already argued that the *causa sui* (in its strong form) requirement seems to be untenable, and the "consequentialist" requirement seems to be too weak. The real choice as far as the conditions of responsibility are concerned is between freedom of will *cum* freedom from coercion (*conception 2*), and only freedom from coercion (*conception 4*).

It should be stressed that from the anthropological perspective (the personalist view of human beings) adopted in this book the problem of whether responsibility ascriptions would be justified if the assumption about the existence of free will were to turn out to be false is purely speculative because the central claim of this perspective is that free will exists. So, from this perspective, the adequate conception of responsibility is *conception 2* (which, obviously, provides a stronger justification of responsibility ascriptions than *conception*

4). But the question of whether freedom from coercion is *sufficient* for responsibility ascription is of great philosophical interest. When one analyzes the requirements of criminal responsibility *explicitly* stated in most contemporary penal codes, one will notice that they include certain perceptual, conative, evaluative, and volitional capacities, but not the metaphysical capacity to act otherwise, i.e., free will. It might therefore seem that penal codes do not treat free will as the condition of criminal responsibility – that they presuppose that freedom from coercion is a sufficiently strong concept of freedom to justify responsibility ascription and punitive practices. Yet drawing this conclusion may be too hasty.[50] One can argue against it in three different ways. One can assert that a *more careful* reconstruction of the presuppositions of penal codes, taking account of not only penal codes, but also judges' opinions and legal doctrine, would reveal that they include also the assumption of free will (one may argue that this assumption is presupposed by the very notion of culpability, or by what is called in the continental legal tradition a "normative conception of guilt"). Furthermore, one can concede that penal codes do not presuppose free will but claim that, if that is the fact, then they are based on a fundamental mistake: They provide a scheme of punishment but this scheme is not sufficiently justified since an agent cannot be held responsible and punished if he could not have acted otherwise, i.e., if he is not endowed with free will. Finally, one can argue that even though freedom from coercion is indeed a presupposition of penal codes and provides sufficient justification of responsibility ascriptions, the justification provided by the free will is much stronger than that provided only by freedom from coercion.

6.2 Accounts of Mental Illness

Let me now pass to an evaluation of the two accounts of mental illness, which constitutes the second dimension of the analysis of the criminal responsibility of the mentally ill. The negationist view seems only partly justified, and, in

---

[50] This conclusion was endorsed, e.g., by Ronald Dworkin (2011: 219–252). He attempted to find the best possible interpretation of our practices of holding people responsible, and came to the conclusion that the interpretation that best fits the data and is axiologically attractive is compatibilism: Responsibility is possible also in the deterministic universe on condition that agents possess "capacity control." Note that the terminology he uses is different from mine: He speaks about "capacity control" rather than freedom from coercion, and about "causal control" rather than free will. But Dworkinian "capacity control" is in fact equivalent to freedom from coercion; an agent has such a control (over an act) if he is conscious of facing and making a decision, when no one else is making that decision through and for him, and when he has the capacities to form true beliefs about the world and to match his decisions to his normative personality (his settled desires, ambitions, and convictions).

addition to that, it is justified in its least controversial part. It is undoubtedly true that certain types of behavior, e.g., masturbation, fellatio, cunnilingus, homosexuality, or sexual promiscuity ("Don Juanism" or "nymphomania") were regarded as mental illnesses (e.g., in the first edition, from 1952, of the *Diagnostic and Statistical Manual of Mental Disorders*) only because they were inconsistent with the then prevailing social norms (all these "disorders" disappeared from the third edition of the *Manual*, from 1980).[51] However, contrary to what Szasz maintained, many other mental illnesses (e.g., schizophrenia) cannot be interpreted in this way. The argument from the lack of evidence for the physical/material basis of, say, schizophrenia, turned out to be the weakest part of anti-psychiatrists' (especially Szasz's) argumentation for the thesis that mental illness is a myth. Szasz may have been right to the extent that at the time in which he proposed his theory the physical bases of mental illnesses were not known, so he could be somehow justified in saying that they do not have such bases. But he should have been more open to the possibility that they may be discovered, at least in part, in the future (as eventually happened; today our knowledge about the physical bases of many mental illnesses, though far from being complete, is large enough to justify a peremptory rejection of Szasz's claim that mental illnesses have no physical bases).[52] We can also put this criticism in a different way. Szasz may have been right in saying that there is no such thing as mental illness *if mental illness is understood in his way – as an "illness" without any neurological/bodily basis*; it may be true that all purely mental disturbances can be interpreted as "problems with living." But the truth is very likely to be, contrary to Szasz's assertions, that this category does not refer to those mental illnesses (e.g., schizophrenia) which are most often invoked in the context of the insanity defense (most of which would have a neurological/bodily basis). Thus expressed, Szasz's claim would be close to tautological: There is no mental illness because illness must, by (his) definition, have a neurological/bodily basis, and mental illnesses, by (his) definition, do not have such bases. Of course, it was not tautological *tout court* because his definition was at least to some extent motivated by an empirical hypothesis: that typical mental illnesses do not have such bases. Yet it was precisely this hypothesis which proved to be false and thus his claim was reduced to a tautology.

---

[51] It should be noted, however, that the new (more permissive) sexual mores gave rise to new sexual "disorders" or "dysfunctions" (albeit not coined as mental), such as anorgasmia, inhibited sexual desire, sexual aversion, or ejaculatory incompetence (premature ejaculation).

[52] It should be added that in one of his latest papers (from 2011) Szasz fully endorsed his position developed 50 years earlier in his *The Myth of Mental Illness*.

Another criticism of this type of theory, provided, among others, by Wakefield (1992), Kendell (2005), and Shorter (2011), concerns his lesion or morphological abnormality account of disorder; as Wakefield noted:

> The account consists of two theses: (a) that a lesion (or abnormal bodily structure) is simply a statistical deviation from a typical anatomical structure and (b) that a physical disorder is simply a lesion. First, the idea that a lesion can be directly recognized by its deviant anatomical structure is incorrect. Bodily structures normally vary from person to person, and many normal variations are unusual as any lesion. Moreover, some lesions are statistically nondeviant in a culture, such as atherosclerosis, minor lung irritation, and gum recession in American culture and hookworm and malaria in other cultures. Therefore, recognition of a lesion is not simply a matter of observing anatomical deviance. Second, and more importantly, it is not the existence of a lesion that defines disorder. ... A lesion can be a harmless abnormality that is not a disorder, such as when the heart is positioned on the right side of the body but retains functional integrity (Wakefield 1992: 375).

However, though important, this criticism is secondary: Szasz's main point was that mental illness *does not have a material basis*, so even if he worked out more carefully the concept of the "material basis" of illness to counter the kind of objection raised by Wakefield, it would still be untenable in the light of contemporary knowledge about mental illnesses. However, as mentioned before, Szasz's claim that mental illness is a myth is true when it is qualified, i.e., applied only to certain "mental illnesses"; in this sense, as argued before, it may help realize Torrey's postulate of making a strict division between mental illnesses that are brain disorders and those that are of a different nature (and do not deserve the attention which is paid to them).

Allow me in this place to digress slightly to invoke a more general argument against equalization models of the responsibility of the mentally ill. The argument states that the difference between the mentally ill and the mentally healthy (downplayed in the negationist account) cannot be ignored in our practice of responsibility ascriptions. It can be developed by drawing on Peter Strawson's (1962) analysis of responsibility which is based on the distinction between various types of moral attitudes. According to Strawson, P can be held morally responsible for committing an offense a if, and only if, the type of act he did (the type including not only outward features of the act but also the mental attitude of the agent) elicits a proper – *impersonal* – reactive attitude (moral indignation, moral disapproval) in most other agents (so that we can speak about the social practice of reacting in a given way to a given type of offense). R's reactive attitude is *personal* when P's immoral act endangers his personal interests; if it does not (i.e., is harmful for people whose interests are not the object of concern for R), R's reactive attitude is *impersonal/moral*. Conversely, an agent is not responsible for an act he did if, and only if, he triggers a specific – *objective* – attitude of excuse/understanding (or rather explaining).

Here we reach a point of Strawson's account which is especially important for our analyses, viz. that reactive attitudes (personal and impersonal) are not only sensitive to the positive or negative attitudes manifested in the behavior of others towards us/others but also to whether these attitudes manifest mental sanity or insanity. In the former case we take, as Strawson calls it, a "participant's view" of their attitudes, in the latter an "objective" view, which is directed at explaining rather than evaluation.[53] This implies that *we cannot forbear distinguishing between the responsibility of the mentally sane and the mentally insane*. The distinction, as Strawson argues, is deeply rooted in the way our attitudes function, although Strawson does not explain *how* deeply rooted they are – whether they are changeable or not. He seems to maintain that the rootedness is genuinely deep, since he says the way our attitudes function is part of "the general framework of human life" (Strawson 1962: 6). Furthermore, according to Strawson, our personal reactive attitudes would not change even if it turned out that determinism were true and we knew that it was true; Strawson deems it "practically inconceivable" that "a general theoretical conviction might so change our world that, in it, there were no longer any such things as interpersonal relationships as we normally understand them" (1962: 4). The same applies to impersonal reactive attitudes, though Strawson's argument for this claim is indirect: He claims that it is harder to imagine the situation in which personal reactive attitudes remain while impersonal reactive attitudes disappear than the situation in which both types of reactive attitudes disappear, since they "stand or lapse together" (1962: 10). Thus, since personal reactive attitudes cannot disappear, impersonal reactive attitudes cannot disappear either. To the question whether it would not be *rational* to suspend our moral reactions if determinism were true, Strawson replies that "it is useless to ask whether it would not be rational for us to do what it is not in our nature to (be able to) do" (1962: 10). On a superficial reading of Strawson's paper, one might assert that Strawson's conception does not have a normative dimension as it takes the social practices of blaming/praising *as they are* and does not say what they should be like. Accordingly, if the practice were different, e.g., sensitive only to the "outward" action, or if we were mentally constructed in such a way that we would regard the mentally ill as capable of participating in normal relationships, then there would be no reason to introduce the "insanity defense" to a legal system. Yet the crucial point is that Strawson seems to deny that it could be different and so his descriptive analysis becomes normative if

---

[53] As already mentioned, Max Scheler (2014), in his analysis of the concept of a person, argued in a similar fashion: If we stop treating an agent as a person, we intend to explain his action rather than understand it as intentional; we try to know the causes of this action rather than understand its sense.

one assumes the plausible thesis that one cannot require change of what cannot be changed. The consequence of this conception for the problem of criminal responsibility of the mentally insane is straightforward: Given the depth of rootedness of the Standard Model in our social practices, one can suppose that other models, if they were adopted, could not effectively function because they are too much at odds with those practices. This argument seems plausible even if we take into account the fact that, as we have seen in Section 4, non-standard models were implemented in some legal systems. This is all the more plausible if we remember that in those jurisdictions where the insanity defense has officially been abolished, it is often introduced through the back door when determining the accused person's competence to stand trial, and the question of mental competence is openly invoked at the post-trial stage of determining the punishment.

7   CONCLUSIONS

After this long "tour" through various models of criminal responsibility of the mentally insane, we have returned to the Standard Model as the most cogent one. This model implies the affirmative account of mental illness and is compatible with *conceptions 2* and *4* of criminal responsibility (the personalist view of human nature assumed in this book implies, of course, *conception 2*, based on the idea of free will). The Standard model seems to gain additional support from Peter Strawson's thesis that the distinction between the responsibility of the sane and that of the insane cannot be abolished because it is "built into" our reactive attitudes (or more precisely: in the way in which our impersonal reactive attitudes function) and cannot easily (or, rather, at all, at least in the long run) be dispensed with. Yet Strawson is less convincing when he talks disparagingly about "the obscure and panicky metaphysics of libertarianism" based on the concept of "contra-causal freedom," i.e., freedom of will (cf. 1962: 23–25). *Contra* Strawson, I have argued that the metaphysics of free will is by no means "panicky" but provides a correct view of human nature, a stronger justification of criminal responsibility, and arguably, it is the only view of man which can justify the retributive theory of punishment.

2. The cognitive component

1 TWO VARIANTS OF THE INSANITY DEFENSE

There are two main variants of the insanity defense: the cognitive and the cognitive-volitional. The first assumes that a perpetrator of an offense can be excused if, and only if, he did not understand the nature and/or the normative (legal or moral) quality of his act, whereas the second one assumes, in addition to the cognitive excuse, the volitional one: that the perpetrator cannot be held responsible also if he could not control/direct his act. It follows from this that the insanity defense always contains the cognitive component and is never confined solely to the volitional component. This suggests that the volitional component is much more controversial. I shall deal with the volitional component in the next chapter; this chapter will focus on the cognitive component.

2 THE INSANITY DEFENSE FROM A HISTORICAL PERSPECTIVE

A quick glance at the history of the insanity defense may be instructive in this context. In the early medieval period, the defense was not fully developed because the dominant conception of legal responsibility was the objectivist or the quasi-objectivist one (similar to *conception 5* discussed in the previous chapter), focused only or mainly on the causal connection between the act of the accused and the criminal consequence. The borderline between civil and criminal liability was also unclear (the compensation was often the "punishment" for what we contemporarily regard as criminal acts, e.g., for murder). The situation changed seriously under the influence of the teaching of the Catholic Church, which paid attention to the subjective side of the crime. As a result, mental illness started to be systematically taken into account in the judgments of criminal responsibility. It was due to the influence of this teaching that English common law started to require, for criminal responsibility, both the presence of the criminal act (*actus reus*) and of guilty mind (*mens rea*). The concept of "madness" was invoked precisely in the context of ascertaining culpability. The problem arose, however, as to how mental competence should be defined.

The first "test" (formulated explicitly in the British legal system by Justice Tracy in 1724, in the case *Rex v. Arnold*) was the so-called "wild beast" test: An agent is to be released from responsibility if he was like a "wild beast" at the time he committed the criminal act, that is, to quote the original formulation, if he is "totally deprived of his understanding and memory, and doth not know what he is doing, no more than an infant, than a brute, such a one is never the object of punishment." Yet this test was very restrictive: It allowed only a small number of the accused to be released from criminal responsibility.

The next test to be mentioned is the M'Naghten rule (also called "the right-wrong test") formulated by the UK House of Lords in 1843 in the aftermath of the process of Daniel M'Naghten, who killed Edward Drummond, the private secretary to the British Prime Minister Robert Peel, leader of the Tory Party, mistaking him for Peel himself (M'Naghten was under the paranoid delusion that Peel – or more generally, the Tory Party – was persecuting him). He was declared not guilty by reason of insanity. But the verdict caused an outcry, which led to the attempt to make more precise the rules governing the insanity defense. The result was the formulation of the M'Naghten rule, which became the law of the land in England and was adopted in several American states. The rule provides that an accused who committed a criminal act can invoke the defense of insanity if, at the moment of committing the criminal act, he "was labouring under such a defect of reason, from disease of the mind, as not to know the nature and quality of the act he was doing, or, if he did know it, that he did not know he was doing what was wrong." Therefore, the rule only recognized those mental disorders as exculpating which have affected the intellect; it implied that an agent cannot be held criminally responsible, if (a) he did not know (because of the defect of reason or the defect of the mind) the nature and quality of the act he was doing, or (b), if he knew the nature and quality of his act, he did not know that what he was doing was wrong. Since the condition (a) is fulfilled rarely (it requires that the agent be completely unaware of what he was doing), most defendants claiming insanity under this rule have asserted that they did not know that their act was wrong. It should be noted that the rule does not state precisely whether it is the moral or legal wrongness (or both) of the act that the defendant must be unaware of in order to be exculpated. This point was and is clarified in concrete jurisdictions. As a rule, the insanity defense is recognized if the defendant is unaware of both legal and moral wrongfulness of his criminal act (if, obviously, the criminal act can also be evaluated in moral terms). This may lead to the recognition of the so-called "deific-decree doctrine"; according to this doctrine the defendant who claims that he committed the crime at the command of God, may be deemed not guilty by reason of insanity even if he knew that his act was legally wrongful. This happened, for instance, in the case *R. v. Chaulk* from 1985 in Canada, concerning two boys who broke into a house and killed its owner; they knew that their act was legally forbidden but believed it to be morally right as they thought it was their duty to rule the world. The court, while considering the responsibility of these two underage criminals (as it turned out later, paranoid schizophrenics), decided that the knowledge of the wrongfulness of an act must embrace not only its legal aspect, but also its moral one.[1]

The M'Naghten rule was criticized as too restrictive (i.e., admitting the defense for an excessively small subset of defendants), ignoring the defects in emotional or volitional capacity, especially the role of the "irresistible impulse."[2] For instance, the Atkin Committee recommended in 1923 that a prisoner should not be held responsible "when the act is committed under an impulse which the prisoner was by mental disease in substance deprived of any power to resist" (Kenny 2012: 39). Later, in 1953, The Royal Commission on Capital Punishment criticized the M'Naghten rule on the following grounds:

> The charge against the M'Naghten rules is that they are not in harmony with modern medical science, which, as we have seen, is reluctant to divide the mind into separate compartments – the intellect, the emotions and the will – but looks at it as a whole and considers that insanity distorts and impairs the action of the mind as a whole … To abstract particular mental faculties, and to lay it down that unless these particular faculties are destroyed or gravely impaired, an accused person, whatever the nature of his mental disease, must be held to be criminally responsible, is dangerous (cf. Kenny 2012: 39–40).

But the Commission was not clearly in favor of the volitional component; as Anthony Kenny put it:

> It preferred the addition of a clause suggested by the British Medical Association to the effect that it should be a defense to a mentally diseased person that owing to a disorder of emotion he did not possess sufficient power to prevent himself from committing an act that he knew was wrong. It thought it would be even more preferable to abolish any such test as the Rules and leave it to the jury to determine whether the accused when he acted was mentally diseased "to such a degree that he ought not to be responsible" (2012: 40).

---

[1] This was possible because the formulation of Article 16(1) of the Canadian criminal code was broad, referring potentially both to the legal and moral aspect: "No person is criminally responsible for an act committed or an omission made while suffering from a mental disorder that rendered the person incapable of appreciating the nature and quality of the act or omission or of knowing that it was wrong."

[2] It is worth mentioning that the notion of "irresistible impulse," as a volitional component of the insanity defense, was first proposed in 1840 in the *Edward Cox* case (Cox attempted to assassinate the Queen Victoria) but it was widely criticized (also by the Queen herself) and soon replaced with the M'Naghten rule.

Nonetheless, the volitional component was at least partly introduced – in the Homicide Act, which was adopted in the UK in 1957. It did not abolish the M'Naghten rule but introduced the defense of diminished responsibility (taking into account also the volitional capacities of the perpetrator – his capacity for self-control), which entitled an accused in a murder case to be convicted of the lesser crime of manslaughter. The defense is to be allowed if the jury find that the accused "was suffering from such abnormality of mind ... as substantially impaired his mental responsibility for his acts and omissions in doing or being a party to the killing" (quoted from Kenny 2012: 40). But it "gave no clear guidance as to the criteria the jury should use to reach this decision" (2012: 40). The concept of diminished responsibility, which allows also for the volitional capacities of the perpetrator (his capacity for self-control), was introduced for some time also in the US legal system. It was contained, e.g., in the Model Penal Code designed by the American Law Institute in 1962; the rule (called also "the substantial capacity test") provided by this code is a kind of combination of the cognitive and volitional (or affective) criterion (the doctrine of "irresistible impulse"):

> A person is not responsible for criminal conduct if at the time of such conduct as a result of mental disease or defect he lacks substantial capacity either to appreciate the criminality [wrongfulness] of his conduct or to conform his conduct to the requirements of law. As lies in this article, the terms "mental disease or defect" do not include an abnormality manifested only by repeated criminal or otherwise antisocial conduct.

It should be noted that this rule differs from the M'Naghten rule not only in that it introduces the volitional component, but also in that it understands the cognitive component in a less restrictive way. It is sufficient for the agent to be deemed insane if he manifests *substantial* incapacity to appreciate the criminality of his conduct, and not, as implied by the M'Naghten rule, *full* incapacity to know the criminality of his conduct. Furthermore, the M'Naghten rule requires that the agent "not know" the nature or the quality of the criminal act, whereas the rule from 1962 provides a less exacting condition: that the agent "not appreciate" the criminality of this act. Thus, even though he "knows" the nature or quality of his act (and thereby is not legally insane under the M'Naghten rule), he may be deemed insane if his knowledge is, so to speak, superficial, i.e., does not amount to the "appreciation" of the nature or quality of his act, since appreciation is a richer concept than that of mere knowledge. Thus, "appreciation" is a more exacting requirement than mere "knowledge": One must know the criminality (or wrongfulness – the Model Penal Code gave state legislators the choice to use any of these two terms) of a given conduct in order to appreciate the criminality of the conduct, but mere knowledge is not sufficient for appreciation. In addition to mere knowledge, appreciation contains some other condition, which may be either epistemic or attitudinal; accordingly, appreciation can be called "deeper knowledge," embracing, e.g., the emotional understanding of the meaning of the act, or "knowledge *plus* serious attitude to this knowledge," or the perception of various subtleties of social interactions which are relevant for the understanding of a given norm and its rationale. Furthermore, the rule from 1962 allows that unawareness may concern only the "criminality" of an act (as mentioned, the M'Naghten rule did not make this requirement precise). This also makes easier the establishing of the insanity: The defendant does not have to demonstrate that he lacked the substantial capacity to appreciate the moral wrongfulness of his act; it is enough if he demonstrates that he lacked the substantial capacity to appreciate the legal wrongfulness thereof. To sum up, the set of cases of "cognitive" insanity determined by the M'Naghten rule is a proper subset of the cases of "cognitive" insanity determined by the rule from 1962 (which, furthermore, also admits the cases of "volitionally" insane).

By 1980 the Model Penal Code rule was adopted by approximately half of the states and by the federal government. Yet the subsequent evolution of the insanity defense in the US legal system proceeded in the direction of eliminating the volitional component. It was criticized for two main reasons: that it implies skepticism towards human agency, and that it may lead to releasing from responsibility dangerous criminals (this last fear was aggravated by the attempt on Ronald Reagan's life by the schizophrenic John W. Hinckley, Jr. in 1982; he successfully claimed insanity using this rule, a fact which caused a considerable public outcry). In consequence, in 1984 Congress adopted a document (the Insanity Defense Reform Act) which substantially narrowed down the scope of application of the insanity defense. This federal test of criminal responsibility, which in fact amounts to a return to the M'Naghten rule, provided that a person is not responsible if "at the time of the commission of the acts constituting the offense, the defendant, as a result of a severe mental disease or defect, was unable to appreciate the nature and quality or the wrongfulness of his acts. Mental disease or defect does not otherwise constitute a defense." The restrictive character of this rule derives not only from the fact that it eliminates the volitional component, but also from two other facts: that it requires the mental disease or defect to be "severe", and that it does not require that the incapacity to appreciate be "substantial" (and, thereby, seems to require it to be total). Moreover, it also shifted the burden of proof, laying it upon the accused. Prior to the reform, after the defense presented a *prima facie* case for insanity, the prosecution had to prove that the defendant was sane beyond reasonable doubt; after the reform, the defense became an affirmative defense: The defendant must prove by clear and convincing evidence that he was insane at the time of committing the crime. As a result of the reform, most states returned to the M'Naghten rule-like tests (modifications consist of the replacement of "know" with "appreciate," "distinguish," "understand," "recognize," or "differentiate"). In short, the irresistible impulse defense has lost popularity in the last 30 years in the US (in those states in which the insanity defense includes both a cognitive and volitional prong it most often takes the form proposed by the American Law Institute in 1962).

Finally, one should mention a purely psychiatric account of the insanity defense – the Durham Rule, adopted in the US in 1954 and abandoned in 1977 (now it is only used in New Hampshire). It specified that "an accused is not criminally responsible if his unlawful act was the product of mental disease or mental defect." Furthermore, it provided that if the defendant (or his defense) claimed that he is not guilty by reason of insanity, the burden of proof was not laid upon him but shifted on the prosecutor (as mentioned, in 1984 the burden of proof was again laid upon the accused). But the "product test" proved to be very hard to apply: It was difficult to ascertain whether an act was a product of a mental illness. This test also gave much power to psychiatrists, which caused the lawyers to protest. They were also afraid that, given the vagueness of the concept of mental illness (and of defective mental state), it might be broadly interpreted so as to include also the most serious criminals (e.g., psychopaths). Furthermore, the test implied that the very fact that an act has a cause, even a cause flowing from mental illness, constitutes an excuse. This claim is implausible since all actions are, in a sense, caused – by reasons – and even if the reasons are in fact sick desires, they are insufficient for deeming an agent blameless if they do not distort the agent's cognitive powers and are not uncontrollable (the desires of a mentally sane rapist or murderer are also, in a sense, sick).

In general, it can be said that in common law systems, especially in the US legal system and to a lesser extent in the British, after a long and complicated evolution, the insanity defense has been finally narrowed down to the cognitive component; the volitional component is either explicitly rejected or treated with skepticism and reluctantly invoked. This approach to the insanity defense is essentially different from the one adopted in continental legal systems, which tend to recognize the volitional component as an equally legitimate part of the insanity defense as the cognitive one. Let us look, for instance, at the Polish regulation of the insanity defense. In the Polish penal code, the "two-component" variant of the insanity defense is explicitly introduced by Article 31:

§ 1. Whoever, at the time of the commission of a prohibited act, was incapable of recognizing its significance or controlling his conduct because of a mental disease, mental deficiency or other mental disturbance, shall not commit an offence.

§ 2. If at the time of the commission of an offence the ability to recognize the significance of the act or to control one's conduct was diminished to a significant extent, the court may apply an extraordinary mitigation of the penalty.

§ 3. The provisions of § 1 and 2 shall not be applied when the perpetrator has brought himself to a state of insobriety or intoxication, causing the exclusion or reduction of accountability which he has or could have foreseen.

Similar solutions were adopted, e.g., in the French criminal code (*Code pénal*), which provides in Article 122-1 that "n'est pas pénalement responsable la personne qui était atteinte, au moment des faits, d'un trouble psychique ou neuropsychique ayant aboli son discernement ou le contrôle de ses actes";[3] or in the German criminal code (*Strafgesetzbuch*), which formulates in paragraph 20 the conditions of "*Schuldunfähigkeit wegen seelischer Störungen* (inculpability due to mental disorders)," by which "ohne Schuld handelt, wer bei Begehung der Tat wegen einer krankhaften seelischen Störung, wegen einer tiefgreifenden Bewußtseinsstörung oder wegen einer Intelligenzminderung oder einer schweren anderen seelischen Störung unfähig ist, das Unrecht der Tat einzusehen oder nach dieser Einsicht zu handeln."[4]

One more remark is in order here. It can be easily noticed that all the above-presented versions of the insanity defense (with the exception of the Durham test) contain a mixed – psychological-psychiatric – definition of legal insanity: The cognitive and (sometimes) volitional capacities must be impaired by mental illness or mental disorder (which means that both the sources of legal insanity and their consequences – the legal insanity itself – are invoked). But one may ask why these causes are invoked at all in the content of the regulation; it is hard to imagine by what other causes the cognitive or volitional capacities could be impaired. But the purely psychological account of legal insanity (i.e., not indicating its sources but only its manifestations) would not be sufficient; if it were adopted, it could be easily abused, so that many more mentally healthy criminals would be likely to invoke it *mala fide* in their defense than happens under the rule of the mixed (psychological-psychiatric) account. The only moot point, already mentioned in Chapter 1, is whether the

---

[3] English translation (by the author): "A person who, at the time of the commission of the offence, was suffering from a psychological or neuropsychological disorder which destroyed his comprehension or his capacity to control his actions, is not criminally responsible."

[4] English translation (by Michael Bohlander and Ute Reusch): "Whoever, at the time of the commission of the offence, is incapable of appreciating the unlawfulness of their actions or of acting in accordance with any such appreciation due to a pathological mental disorder, a profound disturbance of consciousness, mental deficiency or any other serious mental abnormality is deemed to act without guilt."

connection between the psychological and psychiatric elements of the insanity defense should be interpreted as being of conceptual or evidential character.

3 CONTROVERSIES OVER THE COGNITIVE COMPONENT

As we have already seen in the context of the presentation of the historical evolution of the insanity defense, its cognitive component gives rise to various controversies but they are less fundamental than in the case of the volitional one – they mainly concern the problem of how it should exactly be understood, not, as in the case of the volitional one, whether it is necessary. What is not controversial is that the cognitive component, in any of its variants, must embrace two requirements: (a) factual knowledge – the agent should know the nature and quality of his action, and (b) normative knowledge – the agent should know that what he is doing is wrong. In my further analyses pursued in this chapter, I shall be more focused on the second requirement, which involves the complicated problem of moral and legal, or more generally – normative – knowledge. While dealing with this problem I shall concentrate on the issue of the responsibility of psychopaths. By way of digression – not related strictly to the question of the cognitive component but undoubtedly related to the question of the responsibility of psychopaths – I shall also deal with the issue of the borderline between "madness" and "badness," i.e., whether extreme evil is possible or whether it is always a sign of madness. But before passing on to these issues, I would like to make additional remarks about the cognitive component.

First, delusions are the most obvious instance of the cognitive failure that justifies the insanity defense since they lead to exculpatory ignorance (obviously, on the assumption that the agent is not capable of correcting his delusions). But, needless to say, the very concept of delusion generates various controversies, e.g., whether they are (false) beliefs (which are preserved in spite of the evidence to the contrary) or no beliefs at all (because, e.g., they are not integrated with other beliefs and are not responsive to evidence); whether they are perceptual and/or cognitive deficits to be accounted in neurobiological terms (the dominant view) or rather in psychodynamic terms as driven by motivational factors, e.g., by defense mechanisms (this explanation seems more apt with regard to self-deception); whether (if they are assumed to be beliefs) they are always irrational or at least some of them can be considered rational; or whether all, or only most serious, delusions (the dominant view) justify the insanity defense. Furthermore, answers to each of these questions can differ depending on which concrete delusion is meant.[5] However, these controversial issues, broadly discussed in the literature, will not be examined here. It suffices to say that the claim that delusions fall under the cognitive component and justify the insanity defense is rarely questioned. Yet it cannot be excluded that the exact way in which delusions are conceptualized can be relevant for the insanity defense; for instance, it seems that if they are accounted for in psychodynamic terms, they may provide a weaker basis for the insanity defense as it can be argued that the offender was to a large extent responsible for their occurrence.

Secondly, I would like to mention an interesting understanding of the lack of normative knowledge – viz. as a low-level thinking – which I shall use (even if only marginally) in my further considerations. The so-called low-level thinking is a truncated form of understanding of one's own actions: One defines it at a low – concrete, rigid, narrow – level, without capturing its sense (including normative sense) and broader implications (cf. Vallacher, Wegner 1987; 2012). An agent may be unable to think in a different way: In this case he should not be held responsible (this seems to be the case for those who are severely or profoundly mentally retarded). But an agent can also deliberately adopt this way of thinking: For instance, in order to avoid qualms of conscience, he shifts his awareness to low levels of action identification and thereby becomes oblivious to its real meaning.[6] This strategy of self-deception is quite commonly adopted by criminals, especially if their crimes are horrendous – it is a well-known fact that perpetrators of crimes, e.g., guards in German death camps, tended to focus on technical and bureaucratic details of their crimes and preferred to pretend not to understand their real sense and broader implications. Obviously, in the case of self-deception, the agent is to be held responsible for his act.

Thirdly, the notion of normative knowledge is a tricky one not only because it can be understood in a narrow (thin) way (as in the M'Naghten rule – as a mere knowledge) or a broad (thick) way (as in the Model Penal Code – as appreciation), or because of borderline cases (like psychopaths) as to which it is not clear whether they possess it or not, but also because one could argue,

---

[5] The category of delusions is very heterogeneous. It embraces, *inter alia*, e.g., perceptual delusions; delusions of jealousy, of persecution, of grandeur, of being loved by a famous person; Capgras delusion – that one's kith and kin have been replaced by their doubles; Cotard delusion – that one is dead, disembodied; anosognosia – the denial of illness; or somatoparaphrenia – the delusion that part of one's body belongs to someone else. Cf. Kępiński 1974: 85–102

[6] This is consistent with the rules of action identification formulated by Robin Vallacher and Daniel Wegner. One rule says that when lower- and higher-level act identity are available, the agent tends to choose the higher level. But another rule says that if higher-level act identity cannot be maintained (for any reason, e.g., because it arouses qualms of conscience), then the agent will switch to a lower-level identification.

paradoxically, that normative knowledge *is not* the condition of responsibility. This idea seems to be suggested by Richard Holton in the following passage:

> For many moral failings, culpability requires the relevant bad motive. But we do not require that in addition the agent have, or be able to have, *knowledge* of that motive. A person can be spiteful or selfish, or impatient without knowing, or being able to know they are; and such ignorance does not excuse the fault. Likewise, for criminal offenses, the law sets down the appropriate *mens rea*. This will typically require knowledge of certain facts about the external world – that the action was harmful, or likely to be harmful, that object taken was the property of another, and so on – but it never requires knowledge of the very state of mind. It is no legal defense that one is ignorant of one's own motives. People can be guilty while honestly believing themselves to be innocent, just as they can be innocent while believing they are guilty (Holton 2010: 93–94).

Yet the paradox can be easily solved. Indeed, for agents to be held responsible for their acts, they do not have to possess *concrete* knowledge that the act they commit is wrong; criminal and moral offenders typically find some way to morally rationalize/justify their acts (repentance is a rare phenomenon among them). However, they must have *the abstract* knowledge of the difference between the right and the wrong – the knowledge of ethical principles; precisely this kind of knowledge propels them to undertake the task of moral rationalization of their immoral deeds.

4 PSYCHOPATHS AND THEIR NORMATIVE KNOWLEDGE

4.1 The Nature of Psychopathy

Psychopathy is a special form of antisocial personality disorder (ASPD). People with ASPD display a consistent tendency to violate moral and legal norms, to infringe on other people's rights, or to behave aggressively and violently. They are psychopaths if, additionally, they exhibit jointly various other features which are neatly summarized in the so-called triarchic model of psychopathy (cf. Patrick, Fowles, Krueger 2009: 628): boldness (fearless dominance, venturesomeness, social assertiveness), disinhibition (impulsiveness, weak restraint, hostility, and mistrust) and meanness (lack of affective empathy,[7] cruelty and destructiveness, contempt towards others, predatory exploitativeness). As noted by Steven Pinker, "psychopaths make up to 1 to

---

[7] Psychopaths display cognitive empathy (they are capable of recognizing other people's mental states) but not the affective one (they are incapable of emotionally responding to other people's emotions).

3 percent of the male population, depending on whether one uses the broad definition of ASPD, which embraces many kinds of callous troublemakers, or a narrower definition that picks out the more cunning manipulators" (2011: 51). They are responsible for about 20–30 percent of violent crimes. It has been argued that psychopaths tend to commit more "instrumental" violence (cold, purposeful, goal-directed) than "reactive" violence (hot, reactive to a frustrating event, appearing without regard to any good); according to some data, about 93.9 percent of crimes committed by psychopaths are instrumental, and only 48.4 percent of crimes committed by non-psychopaths are instrumental; but it should be stressed that they are capable of committing both types of violent crimes (cf. Blair 2008).

4.2   Arguments Against the Responsibility of Psychopaths

I shall now pass to presenting and evaluating the main arguments for the claim that psychopaths cannot be held responsible for their immoral and/or illegal acts.

ARGUMENT 1: They suffer from neurological lesions.
This argument points to the fact that they have neurological deficits. The deficits are, for sure, to some extent genetically determined, though the extent is hard to measure. As noted by Robert J. Blair:

> The full manifestation of psychopathy is likely to be under considerable social influence. At the very least, increased socioeconomic status (SES) and IQ are likely to mitigate the increased risk for antisocial behavior resulting from the disorder; the individual with higher SES and IQ will have an increased range of activities that may achieve their goals beyond antisocial behavior. However, current data suggests that the basis of this disorder is genetic although the details of this contribution, in which genes are involved, remains unknown (2008: 154).

The neurological research shows that they suffer from amygdala impairment (which accounts for their defective aversive conditioning of fear) and impairments in the ventromedial frontal lobe systems (which account for their disinhibition, poor impulse control, problems with planning, poor foresight, demand for immediate gratification). But, as Nicole A. Vincent remarked, we must be careful with interpreting neuroscientific data, especially those provided by functional imaging; she formulated several "worries and problems with the suggestion that neuroimaging can help us to individually assess people's responsibility." Her "worries" are the following:

> That not all people with abnormal brains commit crimes; that our understanding of how the human brain works is still very rudimentary; that brain plasticity might make it difficult to diagnose who has which capacity ... that we can't go back in

time and check what capacities a person had at the time when they committed their crime; that neuroimaging evidence for a person's incapacity may actually damn them even harder rather than exculpating them; ... that people might be responsible for their own incapacity and thus that they might be responsible for what they do on account of that; that people who know about their own incapacity may be responsible for what they do if they fail to avoid situations in which those incapacities may become a problem (Vincent 2011: 42).

Thus it is by no means clear that the neurological lesions of psychopaths can constitute an argument for their inculpability.

ARGUMENT 2: They do not understand the difference between moral and conventional rules.
Their moral reactions are peculiar, different from the rest of the population. They cannot make distinctions between moral and conventional transgressions, they rate personal and impersonal transgressions as equally severe (cf. Blair 1995; 1997). Let me focus on this first peculiarity. Eliot Turiel (cf. Turiel 1979; 1983; Turiel, Nucci 1978) introduced a precious distinction between moral and conventional rules. Moral rules have an objective and prescriptive force; they are valid irrespective of whether they were enacted by an institution or an authority. They hold universally, not locally. Above all they prohibit harming other people, violating other people's rights, and doing other forms of injustice. Their violations are regarded as more serious than the violations of conventional rules. In short, moral rules are serious, universal, and not dependent on authority. By contrast, conventional rules are arbitrary, situation-dependent, and above all facilitate social coordination. They lack objective and prescriptive force, and they can be changed by the appropriate authorities or institutions. They are usually local – not universally accepted. Their violations are regarded as being much less serious than the violations of moral rules: They do not involve harming other people, violating their rights, or doing other forms of injustice.

But the following question arises: Does the fact that psychopaths fail to perceive the difference between moral and conventional rules provide an argument against their inculpability? It is by no means clear that it does. One could argue that the perception of the infringement of rules as something *socially undesirable*, which they are capable of achieving, is sufficient for holding them morally and legally responsible. The case for their legal responsibility is especially strong because the psychopath knows that his act is illegal and it cannot be said that he does not regard it as such since the assignment of a legal qualification is, so to speak, external. Furthermore, the fact that psychopaths do not grasp the difference between the two types of rules – moral and conventional – does not necessarily have to mean that they perceive all rules as conventional; it could mean they perceive all of them as moral (authority-independent). However, it must be admitted that this latter interpretation is not very plausible; the opposite view seems to be more plausible, viz. that "for them, morality is like etiquette, like conventions about which side of the road to drive on, or like chess: a group of more or less arbitrary conventions that place demands on us only because they have been adopted by a social group" (Prinz 2007: 44). But, perhaps, one should take the middle ground between these two interpretations, i.e., maintain that for psychopaths morality takes some *truncated* form: They can capture certain moral reasons *qua* moral reasons, but not all of them. I shall develop this position at greater length in the next section.

ARGUMENT 3: They cannot empathize with those whom they harm.
One could argue that the fact that psychopaths lack affective empathy implies that they do not really understand other people's suffering and thus cannot be blamed for their immoral actions. Yet this argument is implausible. It is interesting to note that Simon Baron-Cohen (2011) characterized psychopaths by three elements – cognitive empathy, lack of affective empathy, and *immorality*. This very characterization implies that the lack of affective empathy is not sufficient for immorality. In other words, the component of empathy (its presence or absence) does not by itself explain immorality. This objection is confirmed by the fact (mentioned by Baron-Cohen) that classical autistic and Asperger's patients are deprived of both types of empathy but need not be immoral (despite the fact that, unlike psychopaths, even their cognitive empathy is diminished). Also, narcissistic and borderline patients are low on empathy but need not be immoral. Furthermore, the very fact that cognitive empathy – the capacity to understand the other person's perspective – is not only present in psychopaths but also particularly well developed (they are infamous for their manipulative abilities) may be taken as an argument for holding them responsible for their actions.

ARGUMENT 4: They are unemotional.
The psychopath knows that his action is regarded as immoral but he does not regard it as such, or even if he does, he does not have a deeper knowledge of this fact; he does not appreciate it fully. This is due to the fact that he does not exhibit the proper emotional reactions, which may be regarded as constitutive of a deeper knowledge. Blair (1995; 1997) argued that their "violence inhibition mechanism" (the notion inspired by Konrad Lorenz (1996)) is seriously impaired (the mechanism induces agents to suppress, in view of the potential victim's submissiveness, their violent reactions). Ishtiyaque Haji (1998; 2003; 2010), in turn, argued that their lack of (or at least diminished) emotional sensitivity, especially their defective aversive reactions, which impair their capacity for the internalization of moral rules, results in the fact that their "ethical perception" is highly impaired: They do not see the world through moral lenses. This is a strong argument which implies that psychopaths do not just fail to categorize certain options as morally right or morally wrong

but fail to see moral options.[8] Even so, I find this argument implausible, since, as I shall contend in the next section, there are several types of moral reasons which the psychopaths *can appreciate*.

ARGUMENT 5: *They are irrational*.
One could assert, like Paul Litton, that "it is difficult to conceive an agent who has truly an undiminished capacity for rational self-governance yet lacks the capacity to understand moral considerations" (2008: 363). Accordingly, in Litton's view, psychopaths do not have moral knowledge because, contrary to the assumption of the argument, they are not fully rational: They have trouble in learning from experience (e.g., from punishment), they discount future payoffs irrationally, they cannot effectively plan ahead, they cannot reason in a coherent and consistent way. Thus, according to Litton, psychopaths do not satisfy the basic standards of rationality. In particular, they lack the evaluative standards ("higher order" desires) which would enable them to assess and guide their action; as a result they are "wanton," i.e., "act on unevaluated whims and impulses" (2008: 382), and it is difficult to understand their reasons for action – "much of their conduct appears unintelligible to us" (2008: 383).[9] Litton concludes:

> The psychopath's diminished capacity for moral reasoning is symptomatic of a more general diminished capacity for rational self-governance. It is not merely that the psychopath has not internalized any *moral* standards; he has a weakened capacity for possessing any kind of evaluative standards, and that weakened capacity is related to signs of irrationality (2008: 375).

If this claim were right, it would mean that the mental impairments of psychopaths are not only of the affective kind, but also cognitive, and it should come as no surprise that they show a diminished capacity to distinguish moral from conventional violations; they fail to make this distinction because they have impaired cognitive capacities, and, as a result, they cannot properly form moral concepts – they are able to say whether an action is right or wrong, but

---

[8] Many philosophers, e.g., Walter Glannon (1997), accept this view, viz. that it is deficient emotional/affective capacities (e.g., the lack of empathy) which deprive psychopaths of a deeper moral understanding.

[9] A similar picture of psychopaths is presented, e.g., by Duff 1977 and Elliott 1996. They claim that the core of psychopaths' shallow and incomplete moral understanding lies in their deficient practical reason – their lack of adequate standards of evaluation of their actions. On this view, it is not the case that psychopaths have *different* moral standards: they have none. As Anthony Duff wrote, "a psychopath is not a rebel, who *rejects* more conventional values and emotions in light of some favored conception of the good: he is a man who has never come to understand, or share in, this dimension of human life" (1977: 192).

they merely mouth with words; their moral judgments are made in the inverted commas sense – they repeat what others regard as "moral" or "immoral." Yet this argument seems to present an overly pessimistic picture of the cognitive capacities of psychopaths; it implies that their functioning in everyday life should be especially difficult, which is patently not the case. It can therefore be easily reversed: If it were true that their capacity for self-governance is not substantially diminished, then it is not probable that they lack the capacity to understand moral considerations. Furthermore, their intellectual deficits, if they are really true, do not seem more serious than those of autistic children or people with Down's syndrome, and these two latter categories of persons do not have a tendency to act immorally or lack the ability to make moral judgments.

In summary, it seems that none of the arguments against holding psychopaths responsible is really plausible. As a result, one cannot also say that psychopaths are doomed to assume a "low-level thinking"; if they do so, it is because they act in a self-deceptive manner. In the next section I shall discuss various solutions to the problem of the responsibility of psychopaths. In the course of this discussion I shall deepen my defense of the claim that psychopaths should be held both morally and legally responsible; especially, I shall argue that there are types of moral reasons which are fully within their reach.

4.3   Solutions to the Problem of the Responsibility of Psychopaths

The first solution states that they cannot be held either morally or legally responsible.[10] For numerous reasons this solution is hard to accept. The first type of reasons are pragmatic: If it were adopted by a criminal justice system, it could make this system dysfunctional. The second are ethical: Paradoxically, this solution could also be unjust to psychopaths. These two considerations are well described by Stephen J. Morse in the following passage:

> At present, psychopathy is not a treatable condition, so all psychopaths who commit non-trivial crimes would be subject to potentially life-long involuntary civil commitment if they are excused by reason of legal insanity. Such a response would clearly be a potential civil liberty and fiscal problem. Psychopathy is a risk factor for crime, but many might not re-offend despite their abnormality. Moreover, the potential extreme loss of liberty seems in many cases disproportionate to the potential risk to society that many psychopaths might pose ... Finally, civil commitment is very expensive. In sum, the remedy of civil commitment may seem worse than convicting psychopaths. This is a serious practical problem (2008a: 210).

---

[10]   This solution was endorsed, e.g., by Glover 1970, Duff 1977, and Fields 1996.

Furthermore, even though Paul Litton's argument (presented in the preceding section) to the effect that psychopaths lack the capacity for rational self-governance seems to lead to the conclusion that psychopaths should not be held responsible (and thereby should be excused), Litten himself does not endorse this conclusion, pointing to some other practical problems it would entail. He claims, e.g., that they present less of a danger in prisons than in civil commitment institutions (where special, segregated units would have to be created for them), and that public opinion would be unlikely to accept excusing psychopaths; as a result, this solution might undermine public support for the very insanity defense. Litton also considers the idea that "perhaps a psychopathy-excuse should be limited to serious crimes" (2008: 390).

It should be stressed that even though the adherents of this solution usually assume that punishment is bad, and that due to their emotional or cognitive deficits psychopaths do not deserve (in the negative sense of desert) this badness, some of them assume a different perspective: They confer a radically different sense on the assertion that psychopaths cannot be held responsible – they maintain that they do not deserve (in the *positive* sense of desert) to be held responsible and punished. For instance, Jeffrie G. Murphy (1972) claimed that punishment is a good (in the sense that by punishing a criminal offender we respect his moral dignity as a person and recognize his moral status as a responsible agent), and psychopaths, due to their emotional and cognitive deficits, their lack of conscience, and sense of justice, do not deserve this good – they do not have the *right* to punishment. Since a psychopath lacks the capacity to respect the rights of others, he "is in no position to claim rights for himself" (1972: 291). Psychopaths, in Murphy's view, should be subject to therapy because therapy (understood as presupposing that its object is not fully a person) is what they deserve. They cannot invoke any *rights* against treating them in a given way; they may only require that we do not make them suffer. This way of exempting psychopaths from responsibility – by treating them as equal from the moral point of view to animals (which, according to Murphy, cannot have any rights) – would not be quite satisfactory to them (or would it? – perhaps, given their emotional impoverishment, they would be indifferent to the exact justification of their responsibility exemption). Murphy, however, weakens his solution by pointing to the practical difficulty of stating with certainty that a given agent is really a psychopath, and especially that he is a *pure* psychopath (because his solution, if it is right at all, seems to be right only with regard to pure psychopaths), and at the fact that the negation of the personhood status of psychopaths may be less plausible if we assume that society itself (for instance, because it tolerates poverty) is responsible for the development of psychopathic personality (on the assumption that poverty may be one of its causes).

According to the second solution, psychopaths cannot be morally responsible but can be legally responsible, although their legal responsibility should be limited mainly to mala prohibita.[11] This solution has two variants. The first one consists in *all* psychopaths being held legally responsible *only* for *mala prohibita*, which they can presumably recognize just as well as non-psychopaths. It may indeed be true that a psychopath's evaluation of the wrongfulness of various *mala* is highly distorted. As Jonathan Glover wrote:

> Asked to list the worst things a person can do, psychopaths included shooting at beasts with air rifles, turning round one-way street notices, pulling gates off posts, and smashing bottles on the road. The replies of psychopaths were both unusually trivial and unusually specific. Psychopaths, unlike the control group, often seemed unable to give reason for their views. It is hard to avoid the impression that these psychopaths are quite capable of mechanical obedience to rules, but have not developed moral capacities of reasoning and imagination (1970: 138).

But this variant would arguably be too large a concession for psychopaths. Perhaps we should take into account the fact that psychopathy is a matter of degree and assume that an agent with some serious form of psychopathy can be held legally responsible only for *mala prohibita* and those with less serious ones should be held responsible for all *mala* (*in se* and *prohibita*).[12] Yet even this second variant seems overly liberal. In my view, differentiating between the psychopath's responsibility depending on whether he committed a *malum in se* or *malum prohibitum* is implausible. *Malum in se* is also – literally - *prohibitum*, so if it is assumed that an agent can be held responsible for a *malum prohibitum* (which is not *malum in se*), because he recognizes and includes in his set of reasons for actions the fact that it is *prohibited*, he should also be held responsible for *malum in se* (which is also prohibited). A similar line of argumentation was developed by Walter Glannon (although Glannon is generally an adherent of the diminished moral and legal responsibility of psychopaths):

> If the individual can be responsible for violating a conventional rule, and for him conventional rules are identical to, or practically equivalent to, moral rules, then he could also be responsible for violating a moral rule. These two types of rules could be normatively equivalent in that each is designed to inhibit moral wrongdoing and enable an individual to refrain from performing actions that harm others. Even if one insists on this distinction and the claim that a psychopath can recognize actions

---

[11] *Mala prohibita* are those deeds which are morally neutral but prohibited by the law, e.g., parking illegally, and thereby have a character of conventions; they correspond to conventional rules (or rather, to be strict, to conventional wrongs) mentioned earlier. They are opposed to *mala in se*, which correspond to moral rules as distinct from conventional rules (or rather, to be strict, to moral wrongs).

[12] This position is endorsed, e.g., by Morse 2008a.

as conventionally but not morally wrong, he could still be normatively responsible and blameworthy in a generic sense for the actions. He could be capable of recognizing that the actions could not be justified by any normative reason, and on this basis he could be capable of recognizing that the actions were wrong. Perhaps more importantly, the content of the psychopath's mental states in engaging in reactive and instrumental aggression would be roughly the same, regardless of whether he recognizes the rules he violates as conventional or moral. If it is on the basis of one's motivational states and their contents that one is morally responsible, and these states and their contents are practically equivalent in cases where one violates conventional or moral rules, the one would be responsible in either case. (2008: 163–164).

All in all, the solution that the legal responsibility of psychopaths should be limited mainly to *mala prohibita* should be rejected.

In my view, *the correct solution is the one which assumes that psychopaths (whether with serious or less serious forms of this disorder) should be held morally and legally responsible for all immoral and illegal actions*. One can try to justify this view on pragmatic grounds (by highlighting some unpalatable consequence of releasing them from responsibility) or moral grounds (by claiming that the moral knowledge of psychopaths is sufficient).

Several pragmatic grounds have already been mentioned when discussing the first solution. However, it may be advisable to add some other ones. As was aptly remarked by Lawrie Reznek:

> ... at the present time, the costs of classifying psychopathy as a disease are greater than the benefits. There is no cure in sight, and such offenders are better dealt with by the penal system. They are extraordinarily adept at fooling psychiatrists into thinking they have responded to treatment, and so should not be handled in the mental health system. Moreover, it is dangerous to think we can cure psychopaths, to seduce ourselves into thinking we can release them, when experience has told us they only re-offend again and again. We have more reason, then, not to see psychopathy as a disease at this time, but instead as the essence of evil (1997: 243).

I will now move on to moral arguments for this solution. One can construct one type of moral justification relying on the expressive theory of punishment (cf. Hampton 1992). This theory assumes that the negative desert of a criminal lies in his treatment of the victim as inferior, in explicitly or implicitly denying his equal moral value. Now, it can be argued that psychopaths understand the relation of superiority and inferiority and are capable of understanding at least one moral norm: that no human being should be treated as an object. Another type of moral justification, endorsed, e.g., by Heidi Maibom (2008),[13] is that

---

[13] Her arguments primarily refer to legal responsibility; her position on the moral responsibility of psychopaths is less clear, but I think that her arguments substantiate the claim that psychopaths should be held morally responsible as well.

the cognitive and affective deficits of psychopaths are not serious enough to release them from moral and legal responsibility. Maibom stresses the importance of empathy for "deep" moral understanding – the condition of responsibility – and argues that the level of empathy of psychopaths is sufficient to hold them responsible for their deeds. She also aptly noted that

> by contrast to typical insanity cases, murders by psychopaths are almost always instrumental, they are not committed in the grips of hallucination or delusion, or while the person has a particularly tenuous grasp on reality, and had the psychopath's morally disordered beliefs been true, his action would still not be morally permissible (2008: 168).

Furthermore, Maibom brilliantly argued that there are many possible moral reasons for refraining from harming others, not only those which are empathy based and refer to the well-being of others, but also deontological (referring to respect for others' rights, to the categorical imperative, to the notion of fairness), religious, prudential (appealing to enlightened egoism), or perfectionist (referring to the moral perfection of the agent himself, to his dignity or to his fear, as Maibom nicely puts it, of "moving to the dark side"). It would be highly implausible to maintain that none of these types of moral reasons is accessible to psychopaths. So even if we assume that their empathy and emotion deficits are very serious (so that psychopaths' deficient empathy cannot trigger pro-social or altruistic motivation), this still does not substantiate the claim that they cannot truly – deeply – know any moral reasons for refraining from harming others and, more generally, that they cannot know the difference between *mala in se* (moral wrongs) and *mala prohibita* (conventional wrongs). It is therefore implausible to maintain that they cannot understand moral reasons *qua* moral reasons (given the variety of potential forms of moral reasons) and – *a fortiori* – legal reasons *qua* legal reasons, in which the prudential component – the fear of punishment – is more conspicuous than in the case of moral reasons.[14] Thus, as Maibom put it, psychopaths are not mad but bad, and bad character – moral disorder which psychopathy is – cannot constitute an excusing condition under the insanity defense. Let me add that it could only be such a condition if one accepted two assumptions: that they are not responsible for their character or, more generally, "psychological makeup," and that the responsibility for "psychological makeup" is a neces-

---

[14] To be more precise, the question of the dominant type of reasons for action by which the law addresses its citizens will depend to a large extent on what legal-theoretic position one assumes: For a crude positivist, for whom law is a sovereign's order, the dominant type will be prudential reasons – sanctions attached to disobedience – whereas for a *ius-naturalist* the law just gives an authoritative recognition to pre-existing moral reasons.

sary condition of responsibility for one's acts. But even if the first assumption were true, the second seems untenable: The very idea of responsibility (moral and legal) would dissolve if we agreed that one must be responsible for one's "psychological make-up" in order to be responsible for one's acts. One should, additionally, point to the fact that psychopaths have free will, which does not "disappear" or become "suspended" just because the psychopaths have some cognitive or affective deficits (unless they proved to be really serious). So, in accordance with the philosophical-anthropological view of human nature assumed in this book, human beings (including psychopaths) have free will, and it is precisely free will which is crucial for moral and legal responsibility. In general, this kind of non-reductionist – personalist – picture of human nature leads to a more rigorous conception of responsibility (i.e., admitting fewer bases for releasing from responsibility) than those pictures which imply a less metaphysical picture of man and thereby deprive him of the dimension of depth (free will), the fundamental capacity to "distance" himself from his emotions, propensities, and affections.

One may ask whether this last – third – solution is not too rigorous, not overly unjust towards psychopaths. Perhaps it is. But this injustice is an inescapable feature of human justice, especially legal justice. We can only say that, perhaps, from the perspective of a "cosmic/God's eye" conception of responsibility *their moral responsibility is likely to be smaller than that of non-psychopath offenders* (because their moral knowledge has a truncated form: they do not have access to all types of moral reasons).[15] Thus, I endorse the solution according to which psychopaths are to be held morally and legally responsible, although it may be true that from the "cosmic/God's eye" perspective their *moral* responsibility should be diminished. Yet is should be stressed that psychopaths may not be unique in this regard: The diminishment of responsibility is likely to be justified also with regard to many other – non-psychopath – offenders, e.g., those reared in very unfavorable social conditions.

This view on the punishing of psychopaths dominates most criminal justice systems. There are, however, some subtle differences (already hinted at in Section 1 of this chapter) in the exact formulation of the cognitive component, which may influence the way the problem of responsibility of psychopaths is decided. In general, while formulating the normative part of this component (i.e., the normative qualification of the action which an agent must recognize

---

[15] Let me recall the content of this conception: A person P is responsible for an act a he committed if and only if P has free will and his act was *voluntary* (free from internal and external coercion), and his responsibility is a matter of degree; the easier it was for him (given his "psychological make-up") to resist committing a, the higher the degree of his responsibility for a.

in order to be held responsible), we can use either the term referring both to legal and moral aspect, or only to legal aspect. The former solution was adopted, more or less consciously, e.g., in the above Polish penal code, which uses a general requirement of understanding *znaczenie* (the significance) of an action, which can be interpreted as referring both to legal and moral aspect, or in the French penal code, which uses the term *le discernement* (comprehension, discernment). The second solution was explicitly accepted in the German penal code, which uses the phrase *das Unrecht der Tat* (criminality/ unlawfulness of an action) (as was mentioned, the Model Penal Code admits both solutions, as it uses the alternative "criminality" [wrongfulness]). These differences in formulation would be inconsequential if it were generally assumed by the officials implementing legal norms that psychopaths recognize both the legal and moral aspects of their actions. But the differences may be important if this assumption (which, as I have tried to demonstrate, is very plausible) is not accepted. In that case, if the cognitive component requires for criminal responsibility the recognition of both the legal and moral aspect, some psychopaths may be declared not guilty by reason of insanity.

Finally, let me note that one could also argue that psychopathy is not an exculpating or mitigating circumstance but an *aggravating* one. This approach is justified if we agree with Meibom that psychopaths are simply *bad* – their psychopathic condition is a symptom of their bad character, which should be taken into account – precisely as an aggravating circumstance – in determining the length of punishment. There is more plausibility in this view than in the opposite one stating that psychopathy is a mitigating or even exculpating circumstance. But the view defended in this book steers a middle course between these two extreme alternatives: It states that psychopathy is neither a mitigating/exculpating nor an aggravating circumstance.

4.4 Psychopaths and Two Problems in Moral Psychology

The problem of the normative knowledge of psychopaths is connected to the controversy over moral motivation. It is sometimes argued that the case of psychopaths is an argument for moral externalism, and thereby an argument against moral internalism. But whether this claim is right or wrong will depend on how we understand both terms and also the term "moral knowledge."

If we assume that moral externalism is the view that there are no conceptual ties between moral reasons and motivation, i.e., that moral knowledge or judgment is not intrinsically motivating (one may know what morality requires and willfully, not akratically, not act on this knowledge), and moral internalism the view that such conceptual ties exist, then it can be said that psychopaths seem to threaten moral internalism: They have moral knowledge but fail to act on it.[16] Clearly, this last claim only holds if moral knowledge is understood as not including an emotional/affective component; only on this condition can one maintain that psychopaths have moral knowledge, and, since they do not act on it, moral internalism is false. For if moral knowledge is understood broadly, as including an emotional/affective component, then the premise of this argument – that psychopaths have moral knowledge – proves to be false. The lack of this emotional component may not only mean that they are not concerned with morality but that they do not really understand moral concepts, i.e., that they attach to them a different meaning than most other people do. Accordingly, they do not make moral judgments: They make moral pseudo-judgments (for they do not really understand their content; they just recite certain moral phrases without really appreciating their significance). This would imply that they cannot be called amoralists since one can be an amoralist only if one understands morality – if one is capable of passing genuine moral judgments. On this assumption, the case against moral internalism falls. This position is defended, e.g., by Jesse Prinz (2007: 42), who treats psychopaths as a potentially negative "test case" for the claim that moral judgments are intrinsically motivating. In his view, an amoralist – whose almost-perfect incarnation *might seem* to be a psychopath – is a person who makes a moral judgment but is not motivated to act morally. However, he argues that a psychopath does not really make a moral judgment because a person who lacks all emotions but makes moral judgments is impossible. Thus, in Prinz's view, the phenomenon of psychopathy supports internalism and – indirectly – the view which could explain internalism, viz. the view that "standard moral concepts are essentially emotion-driven" (2007: 46). In my view, this argument is not cogent. As I have argued, psychopaths do have moral knowledge since there is a variety of different moral reasons and they seem to be capable of grasping at least some of them. Accordingly, the case of psychopaths indeed provides an argument against moral internalism. That moral internalism may be false does not seem to be any kind of paradox. For, arguably, moral externalism is more concordant with common intuitions: It comes as no surprise to us that an agent may fail to

---

[16] The whole argumentation refers to what Robertson (2001) called "robust" moral internalism, i.e., the view that moral reasons are objective, discoverable, and thereby not dependent on the contingent facts about human motivation. Another version of moral internalism – called by Robertson "attenuated"– assumes that moral reasons depend upon contingent facts about our motivation, and that thereby a loss of moral motivation implies a change in the agent's moral beliefs. On this last version, typical for the sentimentalist current in ethics, the case of psychopaths seems irrelevant: One can plausibly argue that it could not undermine it since a psychopath's failure to act on his moral reasons could be interpreted as meaning simply that his moral reasons have changed.

be motivated by reasons which he accepts; we seem to treat moral reasons and motivation as two different things.

Another problem in moral psychology, inextricably related to the previous one, concerns the role of reason and emotions in moral judgments and moral decision-making. One view – moral cognitivism[17] – asserts that reason alone, without emotions, can make moral judgments, and this rational moral judgment can alone, without emotions, motivate moral action. This can be called a "Kantian" – rationalist (cognitivist) – view of morality. By contrast, moral sentimentalism assumes that a belief can never by itself lead to a moral action; beliefs only have instrumental functions – they are formed to find ways of satisfying pre-existing goals determined by desires/emotions. This is a Humean view of morality. Now, it might seem that the case of psychopaths threatens moral cognitivism: They seem to have some kind of moral knowledge, but they do not tend to act on it. The reason may be that this knowledge is in fact only apparent – due to their lack of moral emotions, which, on the Humean view, are necessary to draw the distinction between right and wrong, and so to make a genuine moral judgment. But one can also argue for the opposite claim: If one assumes that psychopaths do not have moral emotions but nonetheless *sometimes* act morally, then one can contend that their moral action is caused by a moral belief alone. This kind of defense of moral cognitivism seems to me correct since, as I have argued, there are types of moral reasons which can be grasped by those with affective/emotional deficits. It is therefore convincing to maintain that psychopaths have genuine moral knowledge. There is also another way to criticize the claim that the case of psychopaths threatens moral cognitivism. One could contend, like Paul Litton, that they have serious defects

---

[17] Shaun Nichols (2002) calls this view "empirical rationalism." Prinz (2007), in turn, calls it "epistemic rationalism," and the opposing view – that we need emotions to know moral facts – "epistemic emotionism," ; he distinguishes it from "metaphysical emotionism" – a metaethical view according to which there is an essential tie between emotions and moral properties, i.e., moral properties are defined in terms of sentiments elicited by given actions or states of affairs. On this view, e.g., a murder is morally wrongful *because* it elicits negative reactions (of disapproval, anger, etc.), rather than eliciting such reactions *because* it is morally wrongful (Prinz endorses both forms of emotionism). Metaphysical emotionism is a very controversial view (it has, e.g., relativistic implications) but its critique goes beyond the scope of my analysis (for a perspicacious critique of this kind of view see especially Lewis 1943). Let me also note that it can plausibly be argued (cf. Wojtyła 1986b) that moral cognitivism – the view that reason dominates the emotions in moral judgment and moral decision-making – is strictly connected with the objectivist view of morality, implying that there exist objective values (or, to use the classical terminology, that there exists *bonum honestum* (by definition discoverable only by reason), and not only *bonum utile* and *bonum delectabile*.

also in practical reason.[18] This view implies that psychopaths have both intellectual and affective deficits, and thus should not be invoked as a "test case" in the dispute between the adherents of the Kantian approach to morality and the adherents of the Humean approach. At any rate, the problem of whether moral cognitivism (empirical rationalism) is a correct view is complex, and, it would seem, cannot be resolved at the present stage of the development of science. It seems that moral cognitivism could only be rejected if it were understood in an extreme fashion, as implying that moral beliefs may lead to moral behavior without any participation of emotions whatsoever. But this version was not endorsed by even the staunchest adherents of moral cognitivism (e.g., Kant); they all claimed that moral beliefs lead to moral actions through the medium of certain emotions – not preexistent but produced by the beliefs alone (for Kant, this emotion was *Achtung* – respect for the moral law).[19] To sum up, one cannot claim that the case of the psychopaths provides any kind of argument against moral cognitivism. If anything, it seems to support this view: Even though psychopaths suffer from emotional deficits they seem to have moral knowledge and at least sometimes to act on it.

5   THE BORDERLINE BETWEEN BADNESS AND MADNESS

In this section, which is only indirectly connected with the cognitive component of the insanity defense, I shall deal with an important problem of the borderline between "badness and madness" (evil and mental illness). The argumentation developed in this section will provide a refutation of the paradoxical claim that extreme evil can be committed only by the mad, i.e., that the perpetrators of most hideous (extremely evil) crimes cannot be punished, for their crimes are evidence of their madness. I shall also analyze the types of evil (badness) committed by "mad" people, which will also lead me to some reflections on whether any of them is characteristic of psychopaths.

---

[18]   Though, as I have argued earlier, this view does not seem cogent.
[19]   Kant believed that the awareness of moral law should naturally engender this kind of emotion. As for his argument for the possibility of being motivated by the categorical imperative alone, it is twofold. In the *Grounding of the Metaphysics of Morals* Kant appeals to the spontaneity of reason as evidence for our noumenal nature, and thereby for autonomous will; by contrast, in the *Critique of Practical Reason* Kant simply *assumes* that we can be motivated by the categorical imperative, and from this fact of reason he derives his claim that we are endowed with an autonomous will. As we can see, Kant makes a strict link between the capacity to be motivated by the categorical imperative alone and the existence of autonomous will (that is: of free will).

Let me start by distinguishing between three views on the relationship between evil and mental illness. The first view asserts that up to a certain – high – degree (H) of the intensity of evil (the degree at which we can speak about *extreme* evil), an evil action is not a sign of mental illness, i.e., it need not be interpreted as having been committed by a mentally sane offender (though, of course, this non-extreme evil can be committed by the mentally insane!). But once this degree is overstepped, evil becomes so outrageous that it can only be interpreted as a manifestation of mental illness; no sane person could have committed it. And the more outrageous the evil is, the more serious mental illness is likely to be its cause (one word on a question of terminology: I use the term "evil" in a broad sense, i.e., as referring to all forms of wrongdoing; in its narrow sense it is applied only to the most despicable, most serious forms of wrongdoing; if this term were used in a narrow sense, then this high degree of wrongdoing could be dubbed "evil"). The second view implies that mental illness and evil are two entirely independent variables. This implies that even an extremely high level of evil manifested in an act does not mean by itself that the act has been committed by a mentally ill offender. The third view assumes that every instance of evil-doing, insofar as it flows from a certain stable propensity, is a sign of mental illness. The more evil an agent's act is, the more serious mental illness can be ascribed to him. This last view was defended by many ancient philosophers such as Plato or Boethius. According to this view, all evil persons suffer from some kind of mental illness or disorder, and punishment is a form of therapy. As Feinberg pointed out:

> Legal punishment raised a moral problem for Plato that led him to formulate a theory that blended wickedness with sickness. It was his firm conviction that it is always morally wrong to inflict harm on another human being for any reason whatsoever. But if we think of punishment as therapeutic treatment by a moral practitioner who presumably is intent on benefitting (not harming) the person he punishes, we can appreciate how punishment can be a morally acceptable way of treating people, initial appearances to the contrary. If punishment can restore a patient's soul to harmony then by punishing him, we may positively benefit him (2002b: 196).

A modern version of this view is the "humanitarian theory of punishment," which avoids the terminology of the classical philosophy (and thereby does not assert that the goal of punishment is curing the disease of the soul) but expresses a quite similar idea, viz. that the goal of punishment is resocialization. What is common for the ancient and contemporary versions is the assumption that the perpetrator of a criminal act is himself a victim, a sufferer, and thereby is not fully responsible for his action (because he is mentally insane – the ancient version, or because he is the victim of social or biological circumstances – the contemporary version). Therefore, this view rejects the retributive assumption that an agent is punished because he deserved it.

Let me now move on to an evaluation of these views. The third view can be questioned on metaphysical, linguistic, and practical grounds. It implicitly assumes that agents are deprived of free will – the assumption that is incompatible with the personalist view of human being. Furthermore, the theory of punishment this view leads to cannot be, strictly speaking, a "theory of punishment" if we assume, as Clive S. Lewis convincingly does, that punishment must by definition be just: It can hardly be claimed that "therapy" can be just.[20] Finally, as stressed by Lewis:

> the first result of the Humanitarian theory is ... to substitute for a definite sentence (reflecting to some extent the community's moral judgment on the degree of ill-desert involved) an indefinite sentence terminable only by the word of those experts – and they are not experts in moral theology, not even in the Law of Nature – who inflict it. ... They [adherents of the Humanitarian theory] are not punishing, not inflicting, only healing. But do not let us be deceived by a name. To be taken without consent from my home and friends; to lose my liberty; to undergo all those assaults on my personality which modern psychotherapy knows how to deliver; to be re-made after some pattern of "normality" hatched in a Viennese laboratory to which I never professed allegiance; to know that this process will never end until either my captors have succeeded or I grown wise enough to cheat them with apparent success – who cares whether this is called Punishment or not? That it includes most of the elements for which any punishment is feared – shame, exile, bondage, and years eaten by the locust – is obvious. Only enormous ill-desert could justify it; but ill-desert is the very conception which the Humanitarian theory has thrown overboard (1954: 226–227).

Thus, even though the humanitarian theory may appear merciful, it is in fact pernicious since it automatically removes the related notion of rights by removing the notion of desert (or ill-desert), and in this manner deprives man of all barriers against the arbitrariness of "experts" (since the determination of the "therapy" is no longer a moral problem but a psychological or social one). This theory, therefore, "carries on its front a semblance of mercy which is wholly false. That is how it can deceive men of good will" (Lewis 1954: 228). Let us also pay attention to the last sentence of the above quote: If we agree with Lewis that only "enormous ill-desert" justifies the humanitarian theory of punishment (and thereby, in fact, therapy rather than punishment), then, assuming that "enormous ill-desert" is typical of psychopaths, it would imply that they should be subject to therapy rather than punished since they do

---

[20] It is worth noting that the same argument applies to deterrence theories of punishment.

not have the right to punishment.[21] Lewis finishes his critical evaluation of the humanitarian theory of punishment with a penetrating observation:

> If crime is only a disease which needs cure, not sin which deserves punishment, it cannot be pardoned. The Humanitarian theory wants simply to abolish Justice and substitute Mercy for it. Mercy, detached from Justice, grows unmerciful. That is the important paradox. As there are plants which will flourish only in mountain soil, so it appears that Mercy will flower only when it grows in the crannies of the rock of Justice: transplanted to the marshlands of mere Humanitarianism, it becomes a man-eating weed, all the more dangerous because it is still called by the same name as the mountain variety (1954: 230).

The third view is therefore utterly unconvincing. The question is which of the first two views is the correct one.

The answer to this question will depend on whether extreme evil can be imagined as having been committed by a mentally sane person. I shall argue that some forms of extreme evil can be committed by a mentally sane person, while others cannot; accordingly, both views may be correct but for different types of extreme evil. It seems that extreme evil can have five different faces:[22]

(1) It may consist in *doing evil just for the sake of doing evil*. This kind of extreme evil is called "absolute," "pure," "demonic." On this understanding, the harm done need not be very serious for a wrong-doer to be called "extremely evil"; it suffices that he is doing an evil act, even a relatively minor one (like stealing pears in Augustine of Hippo's famous autobiographical example), just because this act is evil. He is indifferent to the other person's suffering, i.e., he does not share it but also does not derive any pleasure from it; what may give him pleasure (as a side-effect) is the very fact of violating moral rules, and this violation becomes for him an end in itself. This category of evil-doers may embrace in fact two different sub-categories: those who have intact moral conscience but nevertheless decide to act contrary to its dictates and those who are deprived of moral conscience. It is unclear which of them are to be regarded as more evil. The argumentation, as noted by Joel Feinberg, can go both ways:

> Perhaps *these* [those acting contrary to their conscience] are the criminals who are the most wicked, since they appreciate the wrongfulness of what they plan to

---

[21] There is a similarity between this view and the view of Jeffrie Murphy (discussed in Section 4.3). But, of course, Murphy justified this view in a different way: not by pointing to psychopaths' "enormous ill-desert", but to their lack of personhood.

[22] I develop some thoughts here which were only outlined in Załuski 2018.

do, and then, in defiance of internalized moral authority, they do it anyway. But then again, this group contains mostly individuals who know what guilt feelings are and are capable of suffering remorse for what they have done. Perhaps, then, an intact conscience, instead of aggravating the wrongfulness of its possessor's crime, is actually a mitigation, making it possible for her to deserve forgiveness and redemption (2002a: 176–177).

(2) Extreme evil may consist in *sadistic wrongdoing*, i.e., deriving pleasure from making the other person suffer. In this case, an agent does not commit evil for the sake of evil but in order to derive pleasure from the sight of the other person's – the victim's – suffering (the source of this pleasure may be the other's pain or the feeling of power over the victim, or both). One can call this variety of extreme evil "sadistic evil."

(3) On the third understanding, an act is extremely evil if it causes "considerable harm to a victim," "is done for no intelligible reason," and as such (i.e., being considerably harmful and done without any intelligible reason) is found by people to be "extremely perplexing" (Feinberg 2002a: 144). I shall call such an evil without any comprehensive motive "gratuitous evil."

By way of a historical digression, it is worth noting that extreme evil in the three preceding senses are combined in Seneca's famous description of ferocious persons – those who "kill the strangers whom they meet, not in order to rob them, but for killing's sake (*occidendi causa*), and men who are not satisfied with killing, but kill with savage tortures, like the famous Busiris [a king of Egypt, who sacrificed strangers and was himself slain by Hercules], and Procrustes, and pirates who flog their captives and burn them alive." Seneca insisted that ferocity is not the same as cruelty:

> This appears to be cruelty: but as it is not the result of vengeance (for it has received no wrong), and is not excited by any offence (for no crime has preceded it), it does not come within our definition [of cruelty], which was limited to "extravagance in exacting the penalties of wrongdoing". We may say that this is not cruelty, but ferocity, which finds pleasure in savagery: or we may call it madness; for madness is of various kinds, and there is no truer madness than that which takes to slaughtering and mutilating human beings. I shall, therefore, call those persons cruel who have a reason for punishing but who punish without moderation (Seneca 2020: B. II, 4).

(4) Extreme evil can also be understood as *non-natural evil*, i.e., wrongdoing which consists in violating the most elementary norms presumably inscribed in our nature by biological evolution, e.g., the norms prohibiting killing our parents, siblings, and children.

(5) One can understand extreme evil as *beastly or brutish evil* – evil that is absolutely horrifying and disgust-arousing for it resembles the actions of wild beasts. This category corresponds to some extent to the Aristotelian notion of *theriotes*. Aristotle characterized brutishness in the following way:

> ... of moral states to be avoided there are three kinds – vice, incontinence, brutishness. The contraries of two of these are evident – one we call virtue, the other continence; to brutishness it would be most fitting to oppose superhuman virtue, a heroic and divine kind of virtue ... Now, since it is rarely that a godlike man is found ..., so too the brutish type is rarely found among men; it is found chiefly among barbarians, but some brutish qualities are also produced by disease or deformity; and we also call by this evil name those men who surpass ordinary men in vice (1947: Book VII, 1145a15–32).

The further passages from *Nicomachean Ethics* devoted to the problem of brutishness are quite complicated and admit various interpretations. The interpretation I wish to propose is that Aristotle distinguishes between two types of brutishness: *brutishness in the strict sense – as a beastly behavior* – and *brutishness as an excess of vice* (brutish wickedness); as he wrote, "and we also call by this evil name those who surpass ordinary men in vice" (1947: Book VII, 1145a31–32).[23] The former embraces truly beastly behavior, which is caused by some disorder in experiencing pleasure, e.g., ripping open pregnant women and devouring the infants, delighting in raw meat or in human flesh, some tribes' lending their children to one another to feast upon, eating the liver of one's fellow man, a man sacrificing and eating his mother, eating cinders of earth (cf. Aristotle 1947: Book VII, 1148b17–31).[24] The latter consists, e.g., in "fearing everything, even the squeak of a mouse" (this is brutish cowardice). Aristotle asserts that brutishness in the strict sense is less evil than wickedness/vice (and – as one can suppose, though he does not say it explicitly – than

---

[23] A different interpretation is defended, e.g., by Katarzyna Marenkowska-Rosół (2018), who argues that all varieties of *theriotes* fall under the notion of an excessive vice – moral vice (e.g., excessive self-indulgence, excessive cowardice, or excessive harshness) or intellectual vice (a total absence of reason). The problem with this interpretation is that moral vice implies sound reason, and many of Aristotle's examples of brutish acts cannot but make us doubt the cognitive capabilities of their perpetrators.

[24] Some of Aristotle's examples of beastly behavior are rather disconcerting and can hardly be regarded as evil, let alone extreme evil: e.g., pederasty, passive homosexuality, gnawing one's nails (onychophagy), plucking out one's hair (trichotillomania). Another disconcerting point of his analyses is the claim that brutishness is found chiefly among "barbarians".

brutish wickedness) but is *phoberoteron* (more alarming). He justifies this opinion by arguing that in the brutish subjects

> it is not that the better part has been perverted, as in man — they *have* no better part. Thus it is like comparing a lifeless thing with a living in respect of badness; for the badness of that which has no originative source of movement is always less hurtful, and reason is an originative source. Thus it is like comparing injustice in the abstract with an unjust man. Each is in some sense worse; for a bad man will do ten thousand times as much evil as a brute (1947: Book VII, 1150a1–8).

Thus, Aristotle claims that brutishness is more "alarming" because of the brutish person's lack of the ability to reason (at least in the practical sphere of action) and thereby to make moral decisions, and because of his beastly motivational mechanism (he lacks a truly human characteristic, which is having a principle of action – *arche* – in itself). There is indeed something extremely "alarming" in the fact that a human agent is not fully human, that its "better part", i.e., reason, is perverted or destroyed (with regard to an ordinary animal no such terror can arise because the animal's lack of reason is something natural, something to be expected: Animals just follow their instincts and do not aim at complying with principles or maxims). On this interpretation, human brutishness is both more alarming than human vice and more alarming than animal brutishness. This lack of the "better part," i.e., reason, could also be invoked to justify Aristotle's second claim, viz. that brutishness is less evil because the lack of reason does not permit a brutish person to be held responsible for his brutish deeds. But he does not do it (at least explicitly) in the above-quoted (quite enigmatic) fragment. He proposes a different explanation: that brutish actions cause less harm to other persons. This second explanation is controversial: On the one hand, it seems plausible because, as noted by Katarzyna Marcinkowska-Rosół, a man-beast, owing to his lack of practical reason, "is unable to undertake targeted, large-scale actions that the vicious man is capable of" (2018: 104); on the other hand, it seems implausible as a general explanation because many of Aristotle's examples of brutish actions do cause great harm to others.

It seems that of these five types of extreme evil a mentally sane person can commit evil for the sake of evil, sadistic evil, and non-natural evil. It is hard to imagine a sane person doing evil "for no intelligible reason." *Theriotes* seems to be by definition mentally ill. There is also much to be said in favor of the view that non-natural evil (violating most basic norms, those having evolutionary origins) is more characteristic of agents who are mentally ill. Let me devote some attention to this last claim, which may seem controversial. I shall start from the interesting observation made by Martin Daly and Margot Wilson:

> In the Canadian data, it is ... noteworthy that 35% of maternal infanticides were attributed by the investigating police force to the Statistics Canada motive category with the clumsy label of "mentally ill or mentally retarded (insane)", versus 58% of maternal homicides of older children. Here and elsewhere, it seems that the sorts of cases that are simultaneously rare and seemingly contrary to the actor's interests – in both the Darwinian and the commonsense meaning of interest – also happen to be the sorts of cases most likely to be attributed to some sort of mental incompetence. ... The state that is called "insanity" invites an evolutionary theoretical interpretation: We identify as mad those people who lack species-typical nepotistic perception of their interests or who no longer care to pursue them (2008: 80).

As Daly and Wilson further note, "a class of homicide that is relatively difficult to reconcile with an adaptive parental psyche – killing an older child in comparison to an infanticide – is not only relatively rare, but also relatively often associated with suicide, alleged insanity, or both" (2008: 80). The other crimes that belong to this class are, e.g., matricides or patricides, though they may differ in the degree to which they depart from the evolutionary interests of their perpetrators. For instance,

> parricide presents itself, *a priori*, as a crime more damaging to the perpetrator's fitness that the killing of a nonrelative, but less clearly maladaptive than filicide of a child beyond its infancy. As expected, then, parricides exhibited an intermediate likelihood of being adjudged by the reporting police to have acted out of mental incompetence: 25% of parricides (35 of 140 sons and 6 of 22 daughters), compared to 41% of filicides, and just 2% of those who killed nonrelatives (2008: 106).

Thus,

> whichever category of homicides is most clearly contrary to the killer's fitness interests is the madder act; it should be relatively unlikely to occur at all, and when it *does* occur, it should be relatively likely to be followed by suicide or an insanity verdict. The obvious example is killing kinfolks: To kill one's relative is madder than to kill one's nonrelative, and is, as expected, both relatively rare and relatively likely to be followed by suicide or an insanity verdict (2008: 267).[25]

---

[25] This observation is confirmed, e.g., by the remark made by the great Polish psychiatrist Antoni Kępiński (1974: 204), who claimed that the hierarchy of values of schizophrenics is often different than that of the mentally sane: A schizophrenic may be more concerned with global poverty than with the health of his own child, or he may be indifferent to the health of his parents but very concerned with the well-being of animals.

In support of their account of insanity, Daly and Wilson write that the statistical data show "the disproportionate number of killers deemed insane among those who have killed close relatives" and that "this prevalence of close relatives among the victims of madmen supports the Darwinian interpretation of madness [as] the loss of normal perceptions of one's interests and/or the inclination to pursue them" (2008: 265). They consider the objection that it is the act of killing of close relatives that underlies the attribution of insanity, so that insanity is a label rather than a description of an objective fact. But they aptly remark that "labeling cannot be the whole story" because, for instance, "there is the parallel between cases in which the killer is judged insane and those in which he commits suicide. Homicide-suicide is a futile act which seems to reflect the same sort of loss or reason or abjuration of self-interest that is diagnostic of insanity" (2008: 265); "Moreover, it is not just insanity attributions *after* the homicide has occurred that are exceptionally prevalent among killers of close kin, but also *previous* psychiatric difficulties and committals" (2008: 267). They emphasize that their point

> is not that people suffering from diagnosed psychiatric syndromes are especially likely to kill; on the contrary, some studies suggest that even diagnosed psychotics are not an exceptionally violent group. Rather, the point of these comparisons is that w*hen* the insane kill, they do not manifest the nepotistic discrimination that is characteristic of sane killers. The lunatic seems not to recognize where his interests lie (2008: 267).

The above analysis of various types of extreme evil and the chances of its being perpetrated by a mentally sane person leads to the conclusion that the second view of the relations between extreme evil and mental illness is correct for sadistic and absolute/demonic/pure evil. Thus, in these cases, badness (extreme evil) does not have to amount to madness. But the first view is correct for the other types of extreme evil: doing evil "for no intelligible reason", being *theriotes*, and - to a lesser degree - doing non-natural evil ("to a lesser degree" because although non-natural evil is characteristic of mentally insane persons, it can also be committed by mentally sane ones). In these cases, badness amounts to – or is at least very likely to amount to – mental illness.

At this point, some final observations are worth making.

First, the idea that extreme evil amounts to madness leads, as rightly noted by Feinberg, to a paradox that "the more wicked a behavior is, the more sick it is. But then we have to declare not guilty the most wicked because they are sick" (Feinberg 2002b: 193); in other words,

> there must be some point in the moral degeneration of a good man when he is just as wicked as he can be, so that as he becomes more and more abandoned to his evil bent from that point on, he becomes less and less wicked, until at the limit of

near-depravity, he is not wicked at all. Wickedness, in short, has a critical point of diminishing return (2002a: 187).

But the paradox is partly removed by the foregoing analysis, which led to the conclusion that there are two categories of "most wicked" (extremely evil) persons who are not sick – these are sadists and perpetrators of absolute/ demonic/pure evil. So even though they are "most wicked," they ought not to be declared not guilty.

Secondly, and by way of a slight digression, it may be interesting to ask a question about the frequency of the phenomenon of absolute/demonic/pure evil. It is worthy of note that scholars even doubt its existence. This skepticism may go too far but, indeed, there are good reasons to regard it as a rare phenomenon. Roy Baumeister forcefully argued that "pure evil" is a myth, which "tends to blind people to the reciprocal, mutual causes of violence" (2001: 94). The core components of pure evil – as understood by Baumeister[26] – are as follows (cf. 2001: 72–74): (1) it involves the intentional infliction of harm on people; (2) it is driven primarily by the wish to inflict harm merely for the pleasure of doing so – an evil-doer is not understood as someone who reluctantly uses violence as a means to an end, rather, the harm inflicted by an evil-doer is gratuitous; (3) the victim is innocent and good – the evil one bears all the blame. Now, according to Baumeister, pure evil occurs extremely rarely, if at all. What therefore causes wrongdoing? Baumeister pointed to several "roots of evil." The first root is a group of self-centered motives, e.g., greed, lust, or ambition. The evil caused by these is purely instrumental: It is a means to an end (pleasure, wealth, power, etc.). Its perpetrator exhibits indifference to his victims; he does not want them to suffer. The second root is egotism: exceedingly high self-esteem. Baumeister convincingly argued that it is a common mistake to assume that violent acts are generated by low self-esteem. He remarked that people with low self-esteem are too depressed and humble to undertake such acts. The violent acts are perpetrated by people with an inflated view of their own worth and importance, especially when this view is not supported by their achievements or personal features (i.e., if their self-esteem is not just high but inflated, i.e., unrealistically high, and thus insecure and easily threatened) – they are both very likely to receive insults, since they require more respect than they deserve, and sensitive to them, since their egos are insecure. Baumeister also links egotism with revenge. However, I think that these two roots should be separated, and revenge (or, more generally, retributive emotions) should be treated as a separate source of evil. It generates evil if it leads to a disproportional retaliation. One of the

---

[26] This understanding is consistent with my own definition provided earlier.

reasons why this happens so often is that people tend to exhibit a certain bias called the "magnitude gap," which consists in victims tending to overestimate their own suffering (losses), and perpetrators tending to underestimate the suffering (losses) they cause.[27] The fourth root of evil is strong attachment to some utopian vision which its believers regard as justifying any means serving its realization (the perpetrator believes that what he does is objectively good). The type of evil generated by this root is called "idealistic." The last root distinguished by Baumeister is the joy of hurting, generating two types of evil: sadism and evil for fun/excitement. As to its frequency, Baumeister wrote that "sadistic pleasure is genuine, unusual, acquired only gradually and responsible for only a minority of evil"[28] (2001: 205); it is "gradually discovered over a period of time involving multiple episodes of dominating and hurting other" (2001: 232). So, according to Baumeister, sadistic evil is a rare phenomenon but not as rare as pure evil.

Thirdly, psychopaths are not *ipso facto* extremely evil in any of the five senses. Their type of wrongdoing was aptly characterized by Joel Feinberg as "moral recklessness," i.e., being "indifferent to the danger he knowingly causes another person" (Feinberg 2002a: 173). But they may also be characterized (in Feinberg's terminology) as "ruthless," i.e., as causing harm to other persons "as a means to, or side effect of the pursuit of something else" (2002a: 173). This last characteristic is confirmed by the already mentioned fact that murders committed by psychopaths usually have an instrumental character. It should also be stressed that psychopaths are not beastly or brutishly evil since, as was aptly noted by Marcinkowska-Rosół, "Aristotle's beasts are not intelligent and ruthless manipulators, but beings whose affective responses and resulting actions (in a certain area of behavior) completely escape rational conditioning, analysis and control, thus resembling the instinctive behaviors of animals rather than normal human actions" (2018: 105). Clearly, psychopaths may also be extremely evil, but if they are, it is not by virtue of their being psychopaths.

6 CONCLUSIONS

Let me summarize the main conclusions of this chapter. I have argued that the cognitive component of the insanity defense is to be understood in a narrow manner – as requiring for responsibility ascription to the agent his *mere*

---

[27] This can be called the subjective sense of the "magnitude gap." It should be distinguished from its objective sense – the fact that victims' losses are usually greater than the perpetrators' benefits.

[28] About 5 percent, according to Baumeister.

knowledge of the nature and quality of the act and of the distinction between right and wrong. This understanding seems more plausible than a broader one, implied by the notion of "appreciation," and thereby admitting a larger number of cases in which the insanity defense is recognized. The notion of appreciation is based on the premise that an agent really understands his act (including its normative quality) if his knowledge incorporates certain affective attitudes. But this premise is implausible. The broad notion of normative knowledge as a condition of responsibility, i.e., embracing also emotional engagement, is indefensible since, as was aptly noted by Reznek, "if appreciating the consequences of one's actions implies that one has sufficient empathy for others (implying that one is motivated not to harm them), every criminal would be M'Naghten insane and have an excuse" (1997: 158). Furthermore, as I have argued, following Heidi Meibom's pertinent remarks, an agent can be said to really understand the normative quality of his act not only if he has a certain affective attitude to it, but also (and this is a sufficient condition) if he can formulate normative reasons for accepting a given rule. And since there are many reasons of this type which do not require having moral emotions or well-developed empathy (e.g., prudential reasons, or perfectionist reasons or categorical-imperative-like reasons), it will rarely be the case that an agent can reasonably be deemed incapable of understanding the normative quality of his act. This was also my main argument for a rigorous approach to the responsibility of psychopaths: I have endorsed the view that they are to be held morally and legally responsible. There is only one variant of the opposite view which I find plausible, namely the variant (defended by Jeffrie Murphy) according to which psychopaths do not deserve to be held responsible (and, consequently, to be punished). Somewhat going beyond the problems of the cognitive component, I have argued for the claim that extreme evil does not have to amount to madness: There are types of extreme evil, viz: the absolute, the sadistic, and – to a lesser degree – the non-natural, which can be committed by mentally sane offenders. In this way I have attempted to solve the paradox that the perpetrators of most hideous crimes cannot be punished.

3. The volitional component

1 THE INTRICACIES OF THE CONCEPT OF WILL

This chapter will focus on the volitional component of the insanity defense and will advocate the thesis that, since the notion of "irresistible impulse" and the related notions of "getting out of control" and "being temporarily insane" – the central notions to this component – are exposed to serious objections, the insanity defense should admit only its very restrictive understanding. The analysis must start from a careful examination of the concept of will. The concept is somewhat ambiguous as many different senses have been attached to it. I shall strive to disentangle them. The basic distinction I propose is between the following two senses: will as a decisional power (hereafter WDP) and will as a post-decisional power (hereafter WPDP).

1.1 Will as a Decisional Power

WDP is a power responsible for making a choice/decision which leads to action; it is therefore the power of initiating an action, "the spring of action" (Arendt 1978: 6). The choice made by WDP is therefore strictly connected to action. It is precisely the will which makes an agent's action his own and justifies holding him responsible for it. The existence of WDP has often been denied but those who affirmed it always insisted that WDP is a *spiritual* and *rational* mental power, a part belonging to a person's spiritual sphere (cf. Rops 1962). Furthermore, it is to be stressed that will is a *power* (*potentia*) and not a disposition (*habitus*). This point is important because it puts the emphasis on the active, sovereign character of the will. This is how will was characterized by, e.g., Thomas Aquinas (cf. *Summa Theologiae*, I, q. 83, a.2). He stressed that this power enables a human person to distance himself from the pressure of his sensual sphere – somatic (instinctive) and emotional (psychic) impulses. He defined it as an *appetitus intellectivus/rationalis*, as distinguished from *appetitus sensitivus – concupiscibilis* or *irascibilis*. Thus, will is a rational power, constitutive of human agency and justifying responsibility ascriptions (since it is thanks to will that our actions are *ours*, that we are their masters, and so they can be ascribed to us).

Let me provide some other characteristics of will. To use the ancient distinction, one can say that will corresponds to *pneuma*, and is "above," i.e., can control, *psyche* (emotions) and *soma* (instincts); to use Hannah Arendt's more contemporary distinction (Arendt 1978), one can say that will (alongside thinking and judgment) is the faculty of the mind, not of the self (which includes, in Arendt's terminology, sensual and emotional impulses, inclinations, desires). The essential, and interrelated, features of will are its capacity to start something new and to act spontaneously (*sponte sua*); this latter feature means that the will is a contra-causal capacity, not determined in its decisions by the antecedent "states of the world," but *beginning* new causal series: Will is therefore, precisely by virtue of being will, *free* will[1] (thus, spontaneity does not mean here unreflectiveness or naturalness, but acting in a free, non-deterministic way). This means that free will and will are one and the same power, though the aspect of will's freedom becomes prominent in the act of choosing – in this case it is more properly called "free will" (cf. *Summa Theologiae*, I, q. 83, art. 4). Accordingly, arguments from the Introduction in favor of free will are also arguments for the existence of WDP (as it is, by definition, free).

One should note that those who believed in the existence of WDP always emphasized its strong connection to reason (which should be clear if we remember that they treated will as *appetitus intellectivus*). This shows that another argument, often raised against WDP, viz. that it implies an artificial distinction between reason and will, is ineffective: The adherents of the existence of WDP themselves admitted that the distinction may be, to some extent, artificial – that thereby reason and will are strictly connected and likely to be two aspects of the same, spiritual reality. This point of view is clearly expressed, for example, in the long quote from *Summa Theologiae* invoked in the Introduction; let us recall its crucial fragment: "Et pro tanto necesse est quod homo sit liberi arbitrii, ex hoc ipso quod rationalis est."[2] And they are connected not just in a trivial sense – *nihil volitum nisi praecognitum* – but in a substantial sense such that rational deliberation is part of the very act of will (though this deliberation need not be conscious). Nonetheless, in classical philosophy the two powers – intellect and the will – though both belonging to the spiritual sphere of human beings, were distinguished for the simple reason that the specific acts are different (cognition and action, respectively). But it should be mentioned that there were many thinkers who claimed that will is strongly independent from reason, that it can be capricious and irrational, and

---

[1] As Arendt (1978: 14) aptly noted, "a will that is not free is a contradiction in terms – unless one understands the faculty of volition as a mere auxiliary executive organ for whatever either desire or reasons has proposed."

[2] English translation (by the Fathers of the English Dominican Province): "And forasmuch as man is rational is it necessary that man have a free will."

that man may find particular satisfaction in expressing his *independent* will against the commands of reason, no matter what consequences it may lead to (this stance was taken, for instance, by the narrator of Dostoyevsky's *Notes from the Underground*).[3] This view of will – as entirely independent from reason, capricious, undisciplined, and recalcitrant – is deeply *unclassical*; it is not part of the personalist view of man, which assumes – let me recall – that will is *appetitus rationalis*: Even if it does not follow reason's commandments automatically (because it is autonomous and not fully subordinate to reason), it manifests a *tendency* to comply with them.

Thus, the following point cannot be over-emphasized: Will is a rational power, something essentially different from instincts, feelings, dispositions, and desires. This means that an agent's acts of will (volitions) are not determined by the totality of his psychological outfit and/or by its motives. The implication of this account of will is a volitional theory of action. On this theory, human action cannot be fully described in terms of desires and beliefs as its causal factors; they play their important role of providing motives and directing action, but they do not lead to action *directly* or *on their own*: The direct cause of action is an act of will. In other words, the action is, obviously, preceded by other mental states (desires, beliefs, etc.) but they are not themselves sufficient to bring about an action. The adherents of this conception are inclined to admit that the concept of volition is hard to operationalize and examine empirically. It is notoriously difficult to identify acts of will independently from the effects (actions) to which they lead (it is a common methodological postulate that causes should be identifiable independently of their effects: If they cannot, then one can hardly speak about the relation

---

[3] A much less radical form of this view was endorsed by the medieval "voluntarists" such as Duns Scotus or William of Ockham. They ascribed to will a stronger power to oppose reason than, e.g., Thomas Aquinas did; but will, on their account, is still, basically, rational – opposing reason is difficult for the will (but its rationality is not full: Duns Scotus, unlike Thomas Aquinas, maintained that will can reject happiness (*eudaimonia*) as its goal, can even hate God, may also at the same time desire contrary objects – in these respects it resembles the will of the protagonist of *Notes from the Underground*). Furthermore, Duns Scotus also emphasized – much more strongly than Thomas Aquinas – will's capacity to resist strong desires; Arendt summarized Duns Scotus's views in the following manner: the will "consists in freely affirming or negating or hating whatever confronts it. It is this freedom of the will mentally to take position that sets man apart from the rest of creature" (1978: 136). Consequently, Duns Scotus, unlike St Paul, believed that "there is an I-can inherent in I-will" (Arendt 1978: 142); the will to do x implies therefore the power to do x. As a result, will should easily overcome various desires and temptations. It should be noted that this kind of view – underlining the primacy of will over intellect and will's strength – leads to an even greater skepticism towards the volitional component of the insanity defense than Aquinas's view.

of causation). But difficulty is not an impossibility: It is plausibly asserted that its existence is confirmed by introspection. Furthermore, if human action could be fully explained in terms of desires and beliefs, then the concept of person (and agency) would be a fiction: The concept of person (and self) would be just a shorthand (and misleading) way of describing the fact a certain psycho-physical entity (human being) is no more than a vehicle for a stream of events (beliefs and desires) which cause him deterministically to act in a given way. On this account the aspects of personhood and agency are lost. It is therefore contradictory to the commonsensical picture of man (to folk psychology), for a part of this picture is not only the claim that mental states (desires and beliefs) are real (and not epiphenomenal) and thereby have a causal power, but also that this causal power is not decisive and deterministic: An additional – executive – operation of the mind, viz. an act of will, is necessary to bring about an action.

The will attests to human beings' capacity for transcendence, which embraces two particular capacities: to distance oneself from one's desires, propensities (the person, unlike other living entities, has an inner life – personal *depth*; spirituality is the condition of interiority), and to be able to direct one's intention to objective values. Thus, owing to our will – one of the signs of our profound interiority – our actions never exhaustively express us; our metaphysical ground – *substance, suppositum* – is always something "more" than our actions and our psychological and sensual impulses. Thus, even though will, by leading to action, most fully expresses the human person, and enables his integration, it cannot be said that actions express the person completely: The person transcends even his own actions. The two aspects of the will mentioned above (being directed to objective values, and being "above" one's actions and psychological and sensual impulses) were especially emphasized by Karol Wojtyła (1985: 175; 2000: 163, 230–234) as typically human capacities (he called them "vertical transcendence"). They strongly distinguish human beings (i.e., persons) from animals, they are "the sign of human spirituality" (Wojtyła 2000: 223) – animals are not directed towards values, and their "actions" are instinctive (animals cannot be said to be "above" them). From what has been said above, it follows that another part of the classical concept of will is being directed to objective values/axiological truths. This feature allows one to deepen the analysis of its aspect of freedom. Will can be free in two senses (distinguished already by St. Augustine): *Libertas minor* (lesser freedom, i.e., free will) consists in the very capacity to choose (in a non-deterministic fashion) between alternative courses of action; whereas *libertas maior* (greater freedom) consists in choosing a morally better outcome; it follows that the morally better the option an agent chooses, the freer he is (in the sense of *libertas maior*). *Libertas minor* is therefore a non-gradual concept, whereas *libertas maior* is gradual. Obviously, it is the former which underlies responsibility ascriptions.

It should also be stressed that will is part of the concept of person, and it is will which manifests itself in – or underlies – a person's two crucial characteristics: self-possession and self-determination (cf. Wojtyła 2000: 151). These characteristics are well captured by the two Latin phrases (the first coming from Boethius, the second from Roman jurists):

(A) *Persona est naturae rationalis individua substantia* (a person is an individual substance having a rational nature). It is precisely by virtue of its nature, which includes a rational appetite which is will, that a person can generate free actions – that he can himself decide about himself, his own actions (this is the precise content of self-determination and, in consequence, of freedom of will; cf. Wojtyła 200: 153).

(B) *Persona est sui iuris et alteri incommunicabilis* (a person is a being of its own and does not have its being in common with any other). It means that the essential feature of a person is belonging to oneself, being master of oneself, who cannot renounce oneself (*incommmunicabilis*) – except, perhaps, in profound love. In fact, self-possession is more basic than self-determination: The latter (which reveals itself in action) is made possible by the former.

Some supplementary remarks on the concept of person and its ethical implications are in order here. The very concept of person has a metaphysical sense and ethical sense: It implies the irreducibility of human being to its merely "natural side" and provides justification for the claim that human beings are endowed with dignity. As such, it underlies an ethical system called "personalist ethics" (cf. Wojtyła 1985: 42). The basic postulates of this ethics are twofold: the negative and the positive. The negative says that person should never be treated only as a means but always also as an end (this is the personalist variant of the categorical imperative); using another person as a means always amounts to treating him as an object – as a something, not a someone, and this treatment may consist either in making use of him to realize some objective end or a subjective end which is pleasure (this second meaning has implications for sexual ethics; cf. especially, Wojtyła 1985). The positive one asserts that each person should be affirmed for his own sake (*persona est affirmanda propter se ipsam*), i.e., the proper relation to each person is that of love (love in the sense of *agape/caritas*, and thus not necessarily emotional love, but love – disinterested and universal – based on an act of will). It is also a part of the personalist conception of human being and of personalist ethics that *the will is not only a psychological fact, but also a task – a challenge; each human being should seek to make his will the root of his actions – the will should dominate the sensual and emotional sphere; the will's potential power should be made actual.* It is only owing to will that man becomes a true master of himself.

In the classical account of will assumed here one more point was important: its *potential* connection to evil. It was argued by St. Bonaventure that human will suffers from *defectus naturalis* (natural defect) – its mutability, which is not by itself a sin (*defectus culpae*) but, rather, *preambula ad defectum culpae* – the first step to sin. As to the source of *defectus naturalis*, he wrote, in a metaphysical vein: "Naturalem defectum voco ipsam defectabilitatem, quae inest voluntatis hoc ipso, quo est ex nihilo."[4] But he stressed that *defectus culpae*, i.e., sin, is not necessarily caused by *defectus naturalis* of will, but by will's freedom: "Voluntas enim non ex hoc peccat, quia ex nihilo, sed hoc ipso quod est ex nihilo est potens deficere" (quotation from Gilson 1958: 125)[5] But St. Bonaventure does not make it entirely clear whether the capacity for sin belongs to the essence of will. This point is clarified in Thomas Aquinas's analysis. The analysis in fact has two parts. Its first is the claim that the capacity for sin is a defect of freedom (will) and, as such, is not part of its essence; it is the feature of higher freedom (God's) that it is incapable of sin (cf. *Summa Theologiae*, 63, 1). In Josef Pieper's summary, the second part (expressed most clearly in Aquinas's treatise *De Veritate*), and similar to St. Bonaventure's remarks about the sources of *defectus naturalis*, reads as follows:

> Not because the will is free but rather because the free will comes from nothing, that is why it is inherent to it not to remain in the good by nature. The freedom may be freedom for the good but not for evil: a free person may be unable to commit evil. A bent toward evil comes to the will not by virtue of its origins from God but because of its origin from nothing ... The creature is dark, insofar as it stems from nothing (i.e., is created). And precisely the fact that descent from nothing is inherent in every creature is the deepest ground for man's capacity for sin, for his *posse peccare* (Pieper 2001: 81).

Thus, man commits evil because he is free (freedom is, so to say, the *almost*-ultimate cause of evil), but his freedom has the potential for evil-doing not because it is freedom (so the capacity for sin does not belong to the essence of freedom/will) but because it is the *defective* freedom of a *created being*, hiding, so to say, nothingness in himself.

From what has been said so far, the impression may arise that will is an omnipotent faculty (which can always easily overcome temptations). But it is not the case: The classical thinkers fully recognized the phenomenon of weakness of will. As was convincingly argued by Hannah Arendt, the discovery of will was connected with the reflection over internal conflicts – the

---

[4] Translation (by the author): "I call 'natural defect' this kind of defect which is inherent to the will due to the fact that the will comes from nothing."

[5] Translation (by the author): "The will does not sin because it comes from nothing; but the very fact that it comes from nothing makes it capable of sinning."

experience described by St. Paul: "For I do not do what I want, but I do the very thing I hate ... For I have the desire to do what is right, but not the ability to carry it out. For I do not do the good I want, but the evil I do not want is what I keep on doing" (Romans 7:15, 18b–19). It is precisely in the experience of *akrasia* – conflict between the will and inclinations/desires – that will reveals itself as a separate faculty; as Arendt wrote: "Freedom becomes a problem, and the will as an independent, autonomous faculty is discovered, only when men begin to doubt the coincidence of the Thou-shalt and the I-can" (1978: 63). However, it is by no means easy to ascertain when the will as a special, rational power of decision-making was discovered (the term "discovery" will obviously be questioned by those who reject its existence – they will prefer the term "invented"). There are some arguments for the claim that Aristotle's concept of *prohairesis* is an early predecessor of the concept of will but, to my mind, the most plausible view is that the will was discovered within Christian anthropology and found its clear expression in the thought of St. Augustine.[6] For instance, Richard Sorabji (2000) argued that St. Augustine (in the treatise *De libero arbitrio*) connected in one concept of will several conceptual clusters which functioned before in isolation:[7] that will (*voluntas*) belongs to the rational soul; that will is *free* will; that will justifies responsibility ascriptions; that one can speak about will-power but also about will-failure (this indicates a close connection between WDP and WPDP – I shall return to this issue in Section 1.3); and that will is present in all actions. St. Augustine's other point was that the origin of bad will (*mala voluntas*) is pride (*superbia*), and that we have two wills – rational and carnal (non-rational) – which come into conflict with each other. This last characteristic was rejected in the further develop-

---

[6] This view was defended by, e.g., Étienne Gilson (1958), Hannah Arendt (1978), and Richard Sorabji (2000). Arendt argued that the Aristotelian concept of *prohairesis* (the faculty of rationally choosing means to a given end) lacks two essential elements of will: autonomy and spontaneity. She asserted that the concept of will was first discovered by St. Paul, and – as was already mentioned – that the discovery (and its further development by St. Augustine) was connected with the reflection over internal conflicts. Arendt (1978: 16) also formulated an interesting hypothesis that one of the main reasons why the will was not discovered by the ancient Greeks was that they assumed a cyclical concept of time, in which there is no place for true novelty and indeterminate future (Arendt called the will "an organ for the future," and regarded it as a source of spontaneous actions, bringing new things to the world). She also claimed that "in the Christian thought freedom is localized in the I-will; in the frame of pre-Christian thought freedom was localized in the I-can; freedom was an objective state of the body, not a datum of consciousness or of the mind. Freedom meant that one could do as one pleased, forced neither by some physical necessity (...) nor by some somatic handicap (...) the basic freedom was understood as freedom of movement (1978: 19).

[7] Though Sorabji himself thought that bringing these separate ideas together was not a good idea; he was therefore skeptical towards the concept of will.

ment of the concept; it does not appear, e.g., in Thomas Aquinas's philosophical anthropology[8] in which will is, by definition, a *rational* power. The related idea of St. Augustine – that will stands behind *each* voluntary action – was also rejected; this idea could only be upheld if one understood carnal will also as will, including various types of desires – anger, concupiscence. Thus, the fullest conception of will was therefore developed by Christian thinkers: They strongly emphasized the *agential, decisive* aspect of will. This conception was described by Wojtyła (1986a: 190) as "dynamic"; and he opposed it to those conceptions of will (he called them "passive") where this agential aspect is either lost or diminished, for instance, Kant's account, on which will is reduced to being an executive function of practical reason, or Max Scheler's account, on which will is entangled and dominated by emotional factors; on both accounts will is not treated as a special – independent and autonomous – faculty; these accounts highlight the causes that have impact on will but not the activity of the will itself.

In summary, whenever we endeavor to understand human freedom, human dignity, human beings' relation to the world of objective values – the building blocks of the personalist (and thus non-naturalistic) picture of human beings – we cannot but posit the existence of a special mental faculty – will – which enables human beings' transcendence (their capacity to distance themselves from their sensual-emotional sphere and to become directed towards the achievement of objective values). It is worthy of note that all the features of human person are related to each other in a very strict sense: If we want to define one of them, we can do it only by referring to the other ones; e.g., free will can be defined as a power of self-determination based on rational deliberation, and rational deliberation cannot be fully described without highlighting its volitional aspect (which is active especially when we compare incommensurable options); or, typically human memory cannot be defined without making reference to will (animals cannot deliberately bring out their recollections: They cannot make "mental journeys to the past" precisely because they lack the will – their memory is not volitional).

At the end of this section, an important objection to the concept of will should be considered. For many philosophers, the claim that will's being free means that it is self-determined – determined by the power of will itself – is

---

[8] Except in some special context – the analysis of Christ's words "My Father, if it be possible, let this cup pass from me; nevertheless, not as I will, but as thou wilt" (Matthew: 26, 39), in *Summa Theologiae* 3, q.21, a.4; as Sorabji writes: "Thomas Aquinas agrees that Christ's will for the cup to pass was not absolute (*absoluta*), but relative (*secundum quid*) to no obstacle being discovered by his reasons. He explains that it was willed not in accordance with the rational will, but in accordance with sensual movements and with the natural will he had as a human" (2000: 317).

paradoxical: impossible or leading to infinite regress. For instance, Gilbert Ryle asked the question of whether volitions are themselves voluntary, arguing that

> either answer leads to absurdities. If I cannot help willing to pull the trigger, it would be absurd to describe my pulling it as "voluntary". But if my volition to pull the trigger is voluntary, in the sense assumed by the theory, then it must issue from a prior volition and that from another *ad infinitum* ... If ... an act of choosing is describable as voluntary, it would have in its turn to be the result of a prior choice to choose, and that from a choice to choose to choose (Ryle 1976: 54, 55).

This objection is similar to the one made by Galen Strawson against the idea of *causa sui*. I have presented several arguments against this objection in Chapter 1. One may also add two remarks to what has been said there: that this feature of will (viz: self-determination) is – as Henri Bergson put it in the title of one of his books – an "immediate datum of consciousness" (*une donnée immédiate de la conscience*); and that it is a specific characteristic of mental faculties (willing and thinking) that they are reflexive, that they "recoil upon themselves" (Arendt 1978: 196), which can be expressed by the phrases *volo me velle, cogito me cogitare*.[9] Arendt adds that cognitive capabilities, like senses or intellect, are directed at the truth (unlike thinking – which seeks meaning), and so "do not recoil upon themselves, they are totally intentional, absorbed by the intentional object" (Arendt 1978: 196). If we agree that will has a reflexive character, then Ryle's objection against the notion of volition fails.

1.2 Will as a Post-decisional Power

WPDP manifests itself *after* making a decision and is responsible for an effective realization of one's goals and plans; it enables an agent to persevere in those goals and plans (self-regulation) and to control their realization by resisting and inhibiting competing and potentially interfering motivational processes (self-control). The role of WPDP is therefore not only to enable perseverance in the realization of one's goals (by facilitating the access of emotions and information that are necessary for the realization of the chosen goal), but also to suppress those impulses one does not wish to realize but which nonetheless impose themselves upon the agent. WPDP goes therefore in pair with such virtues as patience and perseverance. WPDP's existence, unlike WDP, is not questioned, perhaps because it is harder to deny the subjective fact of self-control (and its possible failure) than the subjective fact of an act of will (which one can always try to "demystify" by reducing it to various,

---

[9] "I want that I want, I think about myself thinking"

more specific motivational factors – thoughts, imaginings, desires, acts of attention). Though it should be added that psychologists, while not negating the fact of self-regulation/self-control, prefer to speak about the processes of self-regulation/self-control rather than about the corresponding powers. The latter manner of speech may have for them metaphysical connotations as it implies the existence of some mental power; they prefer the functionalist approach, which focuses on the functions and consequences of the posited capacity; rather than speak about the "power" of self-regulation/self-control, they prefer to decompose it into more specific cognitive, emotional, and regulative processes.

1.3 The Unity of Will

As mentioned, most scholars affirm the existence of WPDP but many of them reject the existence of WDP. However, it seems dubious that this combination of beliefs is consistent. Arguably, the two senses of will are closely related to each other: If one accepts WPDP, and strives to describe its nature in a more in-depth manner, one is bound to reach the conclusion that it is a manifestation of a more general power of "will," which is responsible also – as WDP – for the very act of choice. This view of will is characteristic of the personalist view of human being. There are obviously many detailed questions (belonging more to the field of psychology than philosophical anthropology) which can be posed in order to develop this view in more detail, e.g., what is the connection between the will and the attention? (For example, according to William James, the connection is definitional – an act of attention is a constitutive part of an act of volition: What we subjectively experience as an act of will is the effort of attention to retain and prolong certain thoughts or impressions.); does WDP reveal itself only in complex decisions (in which an agent faces a dilemma, and thereby distinctly formulates two alternative options), or also in simple decisions (in the case of which no dilemma exists)? However, an analysis of these and similar questions would go far beyond the scope of this book.

2   THE OBJECTIONS TO THE VOLITIONAL COMPONENT

Before I begin with a presentation of the objections, let me make two initial remarks.

First, the objections only concern those behaviors which can be called "actions"; if a given action was caused by some form of automatism, then, clearly, it was not an action at all, so that one does not need to raise any kind of defense against it.

Secondly, the first – most general and most fundamental – skeptical argument against the volitional component is provided by the personalist view of human beings and the concept of will implied by it. On this view, the will is the central power of human being, which constitutes its personhood. *The personalist view therefore implies a strong presumption in favor of the effectiveness of the power of will among offenders; it entails that only in really exceptional circumstances can the functioning of this power be questioned.* Obviously, it does not imply that the volitional component should be abolished (this would be the implication of the libertarian but not personalist view of human nature) but it implies that the volitional defense should be interpreted very restrictively, i.e., be allowed only with regard to the absolutely uncontroversial cases (those of serious mental illness). This restrictiveness can hardly be achieved at the legislative level by adopting a "restrictive" formulation of the volitional component (since it is difficult to say how such a formulation should look), but it can be achieved at the judiciary level, in the process of accepting or rejecting the "volitional" insanity defense in concrete cases. The arguments that follow are supposed to additionally support this skepticism towards the volitional component of the insanity defense; the skepticism will not, however, warrant the rejection of the volitional component but rather its very restrictive interpretation.

2.1 The Epistemic Objection

The objection says that it is impossible to state with certainty whether the perpetrator did not resist the impulse (*chose* not to control his behavior) or whether he *could* not resist the impulse (*could* not control his behavior). Thus, the problem is how to distinguish a situation in which a criminal impulse was irresistible from the one in which it was simply not resisted: The incapacity cannot be derived from the lack of actuality. This kind of derivation would constitute the so-called modal fallacy, i.e., reasoning from what has not happened – about what was not actual (not resisting the impulse) – to what could not have happened – about what was impossible (irresistibility of an impulse). This problem is aggravated by the fact that many perpetrators will try to pretend to be mentally ill, counting on milder punishment. This objection was formulated many times, e.g., by Barbara Wootton, or *The American Psychiatric Association*, which wrote in 1982 that "[t]he line between an irresistible impulse and an impulse not resisted is probably no sharper than that between twilight and dusk" (quoted from Erickson, Erickson 2008: 93).

Several pertinent remarks on this epistemic objection were made by Herbert L.A. Hart. He noted that "the philosophical arguments ... pitch the case altogether too high: they are supposed to show that the question whether a man could have acted differently is *in principle unanswerable* and not merely in

Law Courts we do not usually have clear enough evidence to answer it" (2008: 203). Furthermore, in response to Wootton's argument that a man's capacity to resist the impulse lies "buried in [his] consciousness, into which no human being can enter" (Wootton 1960: 232), he aptly responded that the same argument can just as well be applied to the cognitive component – to the question of whether the agent knew the nature and quality of his act: "[A] man's knowledge is surely as much, or as little, locked in his breasts as his capacity for self-control" (Hart 2008: 203). Finally, he carefully reconstructed the main line of Wootton's criticism:

> Her [Wootton's] central point is that the evidence put before courts on the question whether the accused lacked the capacity to conform to the law, or whether it was substantially impaired, at the best only shows the *propensity* of the accused to commit crimes of certain sorts. From this, she claims, it is a fallacy to infer that he could not have done otherwise than commit the crime of which he is accused. She calls this fallacious argument "circular": we infer the accused's lack of capacity to control his actions from his propensity to commit crimes and then both explain this propensity and excuse his crimes by his lack of capacity (2008: 203).

Then, he raised the objection that the evidence for inferring that the agent could not control his action is based not only on the very fact of repeatedly committing the crime, but also on "the manner and circumstances and the psychological state in which he did this" (2008: 204). But his disagreement with Wootton was partial, as he wrote:

> (…) forensic debate before judge and the jury of the question whether a mentally disordered person could have controlled his action or whether his capacity to do this was or was not "substantially impaired" seems to me very often very unreal. The evidence tendered is not only often conflicting, but seem to relate to the specific issue of the accused's power or capacity for control on a specific past occasion only very remotely (2008: 204).

This could be one of the reasons why Hart was not only skeptical towards the volitional component of the insanity defense, but also supported "a moderate form of a new doctrine," i.e., *conception 7* of responsibility (discussed in the previous chapter). I am inclined to share Hart's skepticism towards the volitional component but my skepticism is motivated differently: above all by the personalist view of human beings and by what I call "the non-existence objection" (to be discussed below). As for the the epistemic objection, I wish to note the following.

First, there are three factors which may cause an agent's failure of will: the weakness of the will, the strength of the impulse, and the lack of willingness to make use of one's will. It is difficult to separate them, although the claim that it is impossible would be untenable. It can be done, at least to some extent. If an agent succumbs to a temptation/desire that is hard to resist by most people, then we can plausibly suppose at least "strong impulse." If he succumbs to temptation/desire that is easily overcome by most people, then one can say either that his will is extraordinarily weak, or that he wants to succumb to this impulse. Thus, in this context, epistemic difficulties can be overcome, at least to some extent. But – *and here the strength of the epistemic objection lies* – the transition from the claim about the presence of a strong impulse to the claim about the presence of an *irresistible* impulse may indeed rarely be legitimate; one can hardly imagine data that would justify this transition. What is more, if the non-existence objection, to be discussed in the next section, were right (as, I think, it is), it would mean that this transition can never or almost never be justified.

2.2   The Non-existence Objection

The argument against the volitional component of the insanity defense may go further: One may claim not only that it is difficult to distinguish between "an irresistible impulse" and "an impulse that was not resisted," but also that irresistible impulses do not exist (with the exception of some biological necessities which cannot be postponed indefinitely, like the impulse to sleep, to urinate, or to sit after long standing – the things people will finally do even with a gun to the head), or occur very rarely.[10] It does not mean that the level of ease with which we control our behavior is not changeable; it is clear that it depends on two main factors: the strength of the impulse and the strength of our will. But it hardly ever reaches the level zero. This claim was forcefully made by the psychologist Roy F. Baumeister, who called the notion of irresistible impulse "highly questionable," arguing that people "acquiesce in losing control ..., let themselves lose control and they become active participants" (Baumeister 2001: 274).[11] It is hard to question this claim if one accepts Baumeister's general – and plausible – definition of an "irresistible impulse" as the one which you would follow "even if someone were aiming a gun at you and

---

[10]   For instance, in the case of extreme addiction. Anthony Kenny characterized such actions in the following way:
   If they do cease to be subject to voluntary control, that means that they will be performed no matter how much it is in the agent's interest not to perform them. For to say that an action is subject to voluntary control means that it results from the agent's assessment of the attractiveness of the prospect of the action and its consequences in comparison with other alternatives open to him. If he persists in performing the action no matter what its consequences and no matter what the other alternatives – as may be the case, say, in extreme addiction – then the action is no longer subject to voluntary control (2012: 43).

[11]   Cf. also Baumeister, Heatherton 1996 and Baumeister, Vohs 2007.

forbidding you to do it" (Baumeister 2001: 277). This means that there cannot be many cases of authentic loss of self-control. Baumeister supports his claim by the following observation, drawing on the experience of FBI expert John Douglas:

> After spending his career studying hundreds of serial murderers and other killers, he said there was no way to believe that they were temporarily insane or out of control. For one thing, he noted that none of these killers had ever murdered someone in the presence of a uniformed police officer. Such a murder would be foolish, of course, but if the impulse were truly irresistible, it would not be deterred by the threat of arrest. For another he described several cases in which a serial killer would choose a victim and then cancel the abduction because circumstances did not seem favorable (for instance, witnesses might be nearby). Finally, he said, it is simply implausible that someone who was out of control and temporarily insane could get away with 10 murders without getting caught. Avoiding capture takes too much careful planning and caution for a psychotic or even for an uncontrolled person to manage. Nor are these arguments limited to individuals. Mobs, too, seem to be able to know when to stop (Baumeister 2001: 275–276).

Thus, even if an agent feels a strong desire, leading to a tension and arousal, and to frustration if the desire were not satisfied, it does not mean that the agent cannot control himself; as noted by Stephen J. Morse, "desires and fears of frustration and related feeling states are ... not physical forces that literally force one's body to move if they reach sufficient intensity. They work through the agent's practical reason. ... loss of control is much better understood as a rationality problem than as a volitional defect" (Morse 2002: 1060).[12]

Baumeister also stresses that the level of one's self-control is to a large extent culturally determined; the norms of culture specify how far one can go in expressing one's violent impulses, what impulses one may fail to resist, incurring no moral condemnation or only moderate moral condemnation, when one is allowed to lose one's self-control. As he writes:

> There are ... plenty of impulses that people can learn to treat *as if* they were irresistible. Resisting impulses is hard work, and if people have a readily available excuse for not doing that work, they will often be only too happy to give in. If your culture tells you that a normal and reasonable person would not resist a certain impulse, you may feel free to act it out. This can mean gambling large sums of money, eating too much, drinking to excess – or hitting or shooting someone at whom you are angry (Baumeister 2001: 277).

---

[12] I shall return to the idea that volitional defects may in fact be cognitive – rationality – defects in Section 3.

Accordingly, "the notion of irresistible impulses may be weak and dubious as a scientific hypothesis but as a social doctrine (and as a legal defense strategy) it may be powerful and influential. Once it becomes widely accepted, it is likely to operate as a self-fulfilling prophecy" (Baumeister, Heatherton 1996: 4). This observation is based on their already mentioned plausible claim that the degree of required self-control is determined by cultural norms. For instance, in the southern states of the US, where the so-called culture of honor is predominant, the threshold for the admissible loss of self-control is lower than in the northern states; this is connected with the fact that Southerners are more likely to accept violence, though not violence in general, but "for situations involving an affront, the protection of self, home, or family, or the socialization of children" (Nisbett, Cohen 1996: 38).

Yet it should be mentioned that some attempts at defending the notion of the irresistible impulse have been made. For instance, Lawrie Reznek claimed that "someone has the capacity for restraint if standard changes in circumstances induce him to decide to do otherwise and he does otherwise" (1997: 91). He claimed that a person suffering from agoraphobia will leave the house if the house catches fire, but this is not (in his view) a standard change in circumstances. The problem is, obviously, how to define "standard" change in circumstances. For example, according to Reznek, a threat of punishment is such a change: "If a person would have modified his behavior with the threat of punishment, we conclude he was able to do otherwise and does not have an excuse" (1997: 166). This is an uncontroversial claim. But it dramatically weakens his defense of the notion of irresistible impulse, for the overwhelming majority of potential offenders will be deterred from committing a crime by the sight of a police officer (or more generally: by a sufficiently *real* threat of punishment) and thus should be regarded as having the capacity for restraint.

2.3 The Slippery Slope and the Threat to Formal Justice Objection

Erickson and Erickson highlighted another problem with the volitional component of the insanity defense:

> [W]e enable other types of offenders to offer "excuses" for behavior to escape the criminal justice process ... the numerous novel insanity and diminished-capacity defenses, such as battered women's syndrome gave credence to the fear that the behavioral sciences were excusing behaviors never before conceived as products of a mentally ill mind (2008: 17).

One can add other examples, e.g., the Affluenza Defense, invoked in 2013 to defend a 17-year old teenager from Texas, who, driving a car in a state of drunkenness, caused the accident and death of four persons. The court accepted the argumentation of his family that he was a victim of affluenza – a syndrome of being reared in conditions in which one is not taught that everything is not allowed. This objection can be called the "slippery slope": Once we admit the volitional prong of the insanity defense, then ever less serious "mental defects" are likely to be invoked as causing the volitional failure. As a result, the volitional component may lead to undermining the principle of formal justice: of the equal treatment of equally culpable offenders. It should be mentioned, however, that while these two undesirable consequences of the introduction of the volitional component to a legal system do occur in real life, they occur less frequently than is commonly believed, since

> while public perception may be that the defense is common place, studies suggest that less than one percent of criminal defendants try to use the insanity defense and, of these, only one-quarter use it successfully. A thirty-six state survey found an average of 33.4 insanity acquittals per state, per year, from 1970 to 1995, many of them in misdemeanor prosecutions (Nevins-Saunders 2012: 1419).[13]

Similar remarks are made by Lawrie Reznek. He criticizes four "myths": that insanity pleas are frequent (in fact, they are made in only about 1 percent of cases, and only 10 percent of them are successful[14]); that "the insanity verdict will result in a flood of criminals escaping punishment" (1997: 276); that differences in psychiatrists' opinions are serious; and that there are constant conflicts between lawyers and psychiatrists.

3 CONCLUSIONS

Hart remarked that "the law is ... much more cautious in admitting 'defects of the will' than 'defects in knowledge' as qualifying or excluding criminal responsibility" (2008: 33). This skepticism towards the volitional component is, in my view, fully justified. There are several serious objections that can be raised against it, which I have presented in the preceding sections in some detail. Perhaps they do not substantiate the claim that irresistible impulses (and thereby the offender's incapacity to conform his behavior to legal rules) *never* occur. But, it would seem, they can occur only among those who are *seriously* mentally ill, e.g., suffering from obsessive-compulsive disorder, or among schizophrenics.[15]

---

[13] The author quotes data from, *inter alia*, the paper by Carmen Cirincione and Charles Jacobs (1999).

[14] Note that according to Reznek the "success rate" of insanity pleas is even smaller than according to Nevins-Saunders.

[15] The latter, as stressed by Antoni Kępiński (1974: 193–194), often have a diminished capacity for "integration effort" underlying the act of will "I want."

Three additional observations need to be made at the end of this part of my analysis.

First, the above critique of the volitional component justifies the mixed (psychiatric-psychological) account of the insanity defense. The requirement that the cognitive or volitional breakdown should be a result of mental illness or a defect is some protection against the abuses of the insanity defense (both its prongs but especially the volitional one, which is more susceptible to abuses than the cognitive one), though not a fully effective protection: Mental illness or defect may be ascribed *ex post* as a *mala fide* excuse, especially if one assumes the broad definition – the spectrum/continuum concept – of mental illness (this is another argument, made already in the previous chapter, for restricting the number of mental illnesses relevant for the insanity defense to those which are most serious and have a biological basis). But, at any rate, it is clear that the mixed account of the insanity defense should be preserved. In this context, this account of the insanity defense reveals its superiority; mental illness here has a diagnostic value: It helps to ascertain whether an agent really could not resist the impulse.

Secondly, if it were not only true that the volitional defect can appear exclusively among the mentally ill, but – also – that it is always accompanied (and caused) by some cognitive defect, then it might be reasonable to entirely dispense with the volitional component. But it is hard to unequivocally answer the question of whether the volitional defect/failure can ever appear without the cognitive one. The negative answer to this question was defended, e.g., by Herbert Fingarette, who claimed that

> typically, the Disability of Mind offender has no substantial lack of capacity to conform conduct to the requirements of law. The capacity that mentally disabled offenders do lack is practical capacity to take the relevance of the law into account in shaping their wishes and intentions and in assessing their conduct. The failure may be a matter of emotion, feeling, or mood as well as cognition. The mentally disabled offender, in the typical case, *does* know the nature of his act, knows it is considered as a crime, and *has* the capacity to conform his behavior to law. The trouble is that he wishes to act in a way that does not conform. This lack of intent to conform arises, at least to some material extent, out of his irrationality with respect to the relevant law, and *that* is the ground of his lessened or absent responsibility (1976: 247).

The connection between cognition and volition was also emphasized by Anthony Kenny:

> Precisely because the intellect and the will are not separate compartments it is rash to conclude that a set of criteria like the M'Naghten rules, which are framed in cognitive terms, automatically fail to capture the volitional dimension. The will is the capacity to behave in pursuit of long-term goals and in the light of the comparative attractiveness of alternative courses of action: because of this, an investigation

of an agent's ability to understand what he is doing and its relevance to long-term goals, and of his judgments of comparative value, is not something distinct from, and irrelevant to, an inquiry into the effectiveness of his will (2012: 44).

This conclusion – that an agent cannot control his actions only if he exhibits cognitive defects – seems to hold also on the personalist view of human nature, which assumes that the relations between the intellect and the will are very close. At any rate, it seems that there are few, if any, cases in which an impulse is irresistible and cognitive capacities are fully retained (an example of this type of case, undoubtedly controversial, may be bipolar disorder);[16] the general rule, confirmed by empirical research, seems to be that the main factor regarded by judges as resulting in the loss of volitional control is psychotic delusions (cf. Donohue, Arya, Fitch, Hammen 2008: 65). But since the matter is not entirely clear, it seems reasonable to retain the volitional component, though interpret it very restrictively (only with regard to offenders with serious mental illnesses). Let me make this postulate of restrictiveness more precise: The personalist conception provides the first strong presumption in favor of the volitional capacity; the second strong presumption would be the lack of cognitive impairments. Consequently, the evidentiary threshold for admitting the insanity defense based on the volitional component should be set very high. This conclusion is strengthened by the remark, made already in Section 1.1 of the present chapter, that will is not only a psychological fact, but also a task – a challenge; each human being should seek to make their will the root of their actions. This kind of task would obviously be undermined by an overly liberal understanding of the volitional component, as it justifies or excuses his volitional failures and weakens his motivation to develop his will. Among other things, it can only be admitted if the criminal suffers from a serious mental illness. But it bears repeating that the skepticism justified by the personalist view of human being towards the volitional component is not radical; it would be radical if one assumed, e.g., the voluntarist position in the style of Duns Scotus, who much more strongly than Thomas Aquinas emphasized the sovereign character of will's activity.

Thirdly, it may be pertinent to note here that, as empirical studies demonstrate, the cognitive component of the insanity defense is decidedly predominant in juries' practice (cf. Reznik 1997: 275–276); as Reznek puts it, "the rule that best captures the practice of law is this: Someone is guilty by reason of insanity if he was psychotic and this is causally responsible for his offence"

---

[16] Cf. the following quotation: "Those in favor of preserving a volitional test maintain that debilitating but readily treatable psychiatric disorders, such as bipolar disorder, result in loss of volitional control, while cognitive knowledge and appreciation of wrongfulness/criminality remain intact" (Donohue, Arya, Fitch, Hammen 2008: 60).

(1997: 277). So the lay concept of insanity is "cognitive in nature"; as Reznek stresses, jurors will be inclined to excuse the accused only if he does not know what he is doing. Furthermore, "if a juror judges someone to be evil, then he is not inclined to arrive at a verdict of NGRI [not guilty by reason of insanity] even if the defendant is psychotic [as mentioned the psychotic offenders are most often excused]" (1997: 280). Thus, in Reznek's view, "character is essential to a juror's verdict" (1997: 279); and "juries ignore the legal definitions of insanity operating with their own concept [being a conjunction of two elements: being psychotic and having a good character]. This explains the constancy of acquittal rates in spite of changes in the legal definitions of insanity" (1997: 270). A more precise account of the jurors' approach is given in this passage, which is worth quoting *in extenso*:

> Jurors were not adopting the simple rule: If the man is mad, he is NGRI. Instead, they adopted the As-if Rule, support for the idea that it is *good characters* they are trying to excuse. The As-if Rule helps differentiate those acts which would have been justified given the delusion is true from those that would not – that is, it helps us identify those who are not evil characters. Jurors see themselves as having to answer the question "Is this person evil or ill?" There is an inclination for them to assume that these categories are mutually exclusive and exhaustive, so that if a person is ill, he cannot also be evil, and if he is evil, he cannot also be ill. Jurors judge that if anyone is ill, a psychotic person is, and this inclines them to judge that he is not evil – that he is NGRI. This explains why psychotic offenders are mostly found NGRI. But when a delusion does not satisfy the As-if Rule, showing that the person is evil, this overrides their judgment that he is ill (Reznek 1997: 280–281).

Interestingly, to some extent Reznek endorses this concept, as he proposes a certain re-interpretation of the insanity defense, viz. as "Character Change Defense"; on this account, mental illness constitutes an excuse because it caused an inculpable change of moral character ("I'm not guilty because I wasn't myself when I committed the offense"). But this account is proper only to some cases (contrary to Reznek's conviction, which seems to be that it is applicable to *all* instances of the insanity defense), viz. to those offenders in the case of which mental illness is not durable (so that one can speak about the change of their character), and whose character was not evil before the onset of illness. Certainly, these two necessary (and jointly sufficient) conditions for the plausibility of this re-interpretation are not satisfied in all cases in which the insanity defense can be rightfully invoked. One cannot therefore agree with Reznek that it is the "essence" of the insanity defense that "it is there to excuse those who are fundamentally good characters, and who would not have done evil were it not for the mental illness" (1997: 292).

4 FURTHER IMPLICATIONS: CRIMES OF PASSION

4.1 The Case for Skepticism Towards Crimes of Passion

The above critique of the volitional component can be extended, *a fortiori*, to the so-called crimes of passions or provoked crimes (*a fortiori*, because, by assumption, perpetrators of crimes of passion are not mentally all, and *serious* mental illness is, as was argued, the only circumstance in which the volitional defense can be justified). For instance, in the Polish penal code, such crimes are regulated by Article 148 § 4, which provides that "[w]hoever kills a person due to the influence of an intense emotion justified by the circumstances shall be subject to the penalty of the deprivation of liberty for a term of between 1 and 10 years" (in the case of ordinary murder Article 148 § 1 holds: "Whoever kills a human being shall be subject to the penalty of the deprivation of liberty for a minimum term of 8 years, the penalty of deprivation of liberty for 25 years or the penalty of deprivation of liberty for life").

Let me start my analysis by making two clarifying remarks.

First, one should distinguish between two types of crimes of passion. Crimes of passion of the first type have a utilitarian character: Person A kills person B, not because B did him any harm, but because B is an "obstacle" for realizing A's goal dictated by passion (e.g., creating a relationship with C). Crimes of passion of the second type are different; they do not serve the realization of some life plan; they are crimes of destruction, most often motivated by the desire of revenge: Person A kills person B because B did him some harm. Crimes of passion of the former type are always "cold," whereas those of the latter may be "cold" or "hot."

Secondly, as noted by Eric Posner,

> from a normative perspective, the bare fact that a person acted under the influence of emotion does not excuse his conduct. In fact, while some emotions mitigate guilt, others enhance guilt. Anger provoked by betrayal still mitigates guilt; but anger provoked by unacceptable moral beliefs may increase guilt. Hate rarely excuses murder, but real fear, even if not fully justified, might mitigate culpability (2000: 4).

Thus, in Posner's view, hate (and also disgust) are aggravating circumstances, and anger or fear can be (on certain occasions) mitigating circumstances. Now, in my analysis I shall be focused only on the former, or more precisely, on "emotions justified by circumstances," as the Polish penal code puts it – the only ones that can (potentially at least) justify a milder treatment of offenders committing crimes of passion.

The critique of crimes of passion I wish to make will not lead to the postulate of eliminating this type of "mitigating circumstance" from penal codes, since diminished self-control is not the only reason why crimes of passion were introduced; the other reason is that they may be justified *to some extent*, at least in a moral sense (here the borderline between justifications and excuses – two types of legal defenses – becomes blurred). But the strength of the mitigation should be decreased insofar as it is motivated by the belief that the perpetrator of the crime of passion could hardly control himself. In fact, as was argued, the lack of voluntary control is much less probable, or perhaps impossible, among the mentally healthy.

Let me start my argumentation from the crucial point that there are two different ways of conceptualizing emotions. The non-cognitive theory asserts that emotions are irrational mental states, visceral reactions either entirely deprived of the cognitive component or preserving it in only some very truncated form. By contrast, the cognitive theory treats emotions as triggered by beliefs. Empirical research has not resolved the question of which of them is the correct one. In my analysis I assume cognitive theory to be correct as it is implied by the personalist view of human being, which, let me recall, emphasizes the spiritual part of human beings (reason and will) by virtue of which they are capable of "distancing" themselves from their passions, inclinations, and dispositions. This theory should be presented in some more detail. Following Robert Nozick, I assume that each emotion has three components: belief, evaluation, and feeling (1990: 87–98). A belief may be assessed (depending on the assumed epistemological conception) as true or false, or justified or unjustified; an evaluation may be assessed as correct or incorrect; and feeling (psycho-physiological arousal) may be assessed as proportionate or disproportionate (to an evaluation). From the above it follows that a given emotion can be defective, inappropriate, i.e., *intrinsically irrational* (my, not Nozick's, term) in three ways: Belief may be false or unjustified, evaluation may be incorrect, and feeling may be disproportionate to evaluation (exceedingly intense or not sufficiently intense). Nozick noted that an agent whose emotion is appropriate (intrinsically rational) "responds" to reality in a proper way, i.e., his response is consistent with the "reality principle": Such an agent has an adequate picture of reality encoded in his emotion and his emotion enables him to be closely connected to – "cling to" – this reality (Nozick also stressed that such a response is itself a value, which he calls "a second-order value"). The crucial point of the cognitive theory is its implication that emotions are controllable, that there is no "point of no return" in experiencing emotions at which they inevitably lead to its typical action.[17] Thus, according to the cognitive theory, *we are responsible for our emotions*. This responsibility is grounded in three main facts. The first one is that we can shape our emotions by shaping our beliefs (factual and evaluative): The ethics of emotions is therefore based on the ethics of beliefs. The second one is that if we have sufficient self-knowledge (another requirement of the ethics of beliefs), we can anticipate our emotions, and, consequently, either endorse them or prevent them from developing. The third one is that while it is true that emotions cause a change in people's preferences (and thereby elicit their temporary preferences) and beliefs (e.g., fear may lead to overestimating the probability of danger), it remains the fact that people still act rationally (given these new beliefs and preferences); thus, instrumental rationality is preserved, and thereby the capacity for self-control; as Posner put it:

> people remain rational during the emotion state, so that their behavior will bear some resemblance to calm-state behavior, and remain responsive to incentives; people can anticipate and plan around their emotions, by cultivating dispositions and avoiding stimuli ... An angry, disgusted, fearful or sad person usually can deliberate about his behavior and does not (with the possible exception of certain kinds of fear) engage in reflexive action (2000: 4).

Yet these arguments for the responsibility for our emotions and emotion-propelled actions may not be convincing for everyone. One could object that emotions in some circumstances should constitute a mitigating circumstance; as was argued by Posner:

> It makes more sense to punish people who are provoked into anger by someone they hate and could avoid than to punish people who are provoked into anger during a random encounter with a stranger. The former are in a better position during their calm state to avoid the encounter, and it is during the calm state that they are most responsive .... Whether or not a person's emotional state excuses his conduct depends on whether the person could have avoided the emotion or avoided the stimulus that provoked the emotion and whether the emotion reflects acceptable moral beliefs about others and the world (2000: 4).

He developed these thoughts in the following manner:

> It makes sense to reduce the sanction for an act committed during an emotion state if (1) the emotion is anger (or another emotion that causes people to injure others, like fear, possibly) and it is quite intense, so that high expected sanctions cannot

---

[17] *A fortiori*, this theory leads to the rejection of the view that the "point of no return" is earlier on the scale of the strength of emotions than the point of earliest detection.

deter the behavior, and (2) sanctions are costly, which they are when they involve imprisonment. The justification is that expensive sanctions should not be wasted on people who cannot be deterred by them ... the strongest case for reducing criminal punishment on deterrence grounds occurs when the agent cannot be easily deterred in the emotion state and cannot easily avoid the emotion state either by avoiding the stimulus or changing his temperament. The emotion has to be the right type (anger or fear, typically) and it must be intense. When these conditions are not met, the case for reducing the punishment is weaker (2000:14–15).

Let me first note that Posner seems to assume implicitly a conception of criminal responsibility – by itself controversial – according to which the degree of an agent's responsibility for an act *a* depends on how easily he can be deterred by legal sanctions from performing this act: The easier deterrence is, the higher responsibility is (this is a variant of *conception 6* from among those analyzed in Chapter 1). More importantly, this kind of gradation of responsibility does not seem to be justified by the cognitive theory of emotions (assumed here, not by Posner). This theory implies that we are *all* endowed with cognitive-volitional capacity to *overcome* undesirable emotions, at least in the sense of preventing them from developing into fully fledged emotions, with their corresponding action tendencies; appearances notwithstanding, individual differences are in this respect negligible (it is a matter of choice, for which we can be held responsible, whether we cultivate this capacity or not).[18]

In my view, the subtleties of the gradation of responsibility can only be taken into account within the "cosmic/God's eyes" (I shall return to this point in the next section).

---

[18] Interestingly, Posner's own remarks often go in the same direction, for instance, when he writes about the cultivation of emotions:
   People are self-conscious and generally (though not always) knowledgeable about their emotional dispositions, recognize when these emotional dispositions lead them astray, and take steps to modify them. The idea of cultivating (benign) emotions or even emotionless calm is similar to the simpler act of avoiding stimuli of destructive emotions. A person might seek to control his anger or envy through meditation, yoga, religious pursuits, and so forth; or by avoidance: he might stop going to bars where people slight him; he might move away from cities or neighborhoods where conspicuous consumption is the norm; he might avoid homeless people. In these cases, the person avoids stimuli of anger, envy, or pity that might get him trouble or simply be unpleasant to experience. Cultivation of emotional dispositions and simple avoidance are, of course, very different behaviors, but they can be usefully treated as the same for purpose of analysis (2000: 7).

4.2 Some Historical Remarks on Crimes of Passion

The history of the approach to "crimes of passion" is very instructive. For a long time, crimes of passion were treated leniently if they were committed by men. This was caused by a patriarchal culture which assumed masculine supremacy and treated a woman almost as the property of her husband. Let me develop this point in more detail, looking at its biological and social causes.

From an evolutionary perspective, men's fear of female infidelity and uncertain paternity resulted in possessive behavior towards women and found its expression in the law, which provided severe punishment for unfaithful wives, treated female adultery as a property violation, valued female chastity, allowed or even ordered various types of surgery (such as infibulation and clitoridectomy) aimed at decreasing women's capacity to experience sexual pleasure, and – which is important for the analysis pursued here – recognized infidelity as an exculpatory provocation to violence. One can therefore say that stronger moral and legal condemnation of women's infidelity and treating it as an exculpating or mitigating circumstance in the case of men's violent behavior is a direct expression of evolutionary ethics – of the evolutionarily determined value judgment that the greater blame, because of its negative consequences for the other side, is to be attributed to a wife's adultery rather than to a husband's. As a result, the husband was granted the right to punish and "correct" his wife. It is paradoxical that even though a woman was considered to be a "weaker sex," unable to fully control herself, it was men who were treated leniently when they were carried away by their emotions and killed their wives. This paradox can at least partly be explained by the fact that it was believed (wrongly) that women commit "maricide" usually with premeditation, whereas the killing of wives ("uxoricide") is usually done under the influence of passion (cf. Toure 2007). This approach to crimes of passion was additionally reinforced by the 19th-century literature, which "romanticized" crimes of passion, often showing husbands as having noble motives, deeply loving their wives, and being manipulated by them (as, e.g., in *The Kreutzer Sonata* by Leo Tolstoy). This lenient approach towards husbands committing crimes of passion on their wives can also be noted in the 19th-century criminological works, e.g., of Cesare Lombroso or Enrico Ferri. Ferri (2004: 240–243) presented husbands committing crimes of passion as hypersensitive persons, being often victims of social environment, whereas Lombroso (1991: 405–420) claimed that perversity and premeditation is more prevalent in female crimes of passion. But the approach started to change in the 20th century, with the (slow) demise of the patriarchal culture, and the concomitant emancipation of women. The change was also influenced by psychological and criminological works, which "demystified" male crimes of passion. For instance, Léon Rabinowicz (1931) maintained that these crimes do not flow from noble, romantic motives (deep love), but from low and savage ones, such as "la haine atroce, l'égoisme effréné, l'esprit vil de la vengeance"[19] (1931: 150), and are often premeditated. He claimed that the type of love which stands behind crimes of passion is of the lowest kind: It is sexual love (as opposed to affective or platonic), which is egoist, jealous, and possessive. Accordingly, crimes of passion are not crimes of love but sexual crimes. As a result he postulated the elimination of a category of crimes of passion (more leniently treated than other crimes) from penal codes.[20] This bleak picture of male crimes of passion seems to be confirmed by modern research, which shows that those who commit them are often narcissistic, interpret the infidelity of their wives or partners in terms of humiliation, or as an attack on their virility (cf. Toure 2007). But, in many countries, it took a long time to introduce full change; for instance, in France it was not until 1975 (the reform of divorce and the depenalization of adultery) that Article 324, providing an excuse for a husband killing his adulterous wife (or her lover) caught *in flagrante delicto* in their marital home (*la maison conjugale*), was repealed.

The changes in the approach to the crime of rape confirm this trend of diminished tolerance for crimes of passion. In her analysis of date rape, Lois Pinzeau (1989) forcefully criticized the claim that there may exist irresistible impulses. She rejected the oft-made defense of rapists that they were provoked, and as a result, due to insistent and irresistible sexual impulses, could not refrain from coercing a woman into a sexual intercourse. She very convincingly argued that this kind of defense is based on three myths: the belief "in the especially insistent nature of male sexuality, (...) an insistence that lies at the foot of natural male aggression and which is hard to contain" (1989: 455); the belief that women are sexual "desirers" but are expected to be sexual "deniers," i.e., that "women both want to indulge sexually and are inclined to sacrifice the desire for higher ends [which] gives rise to the myth that they want to be raped" (1989: 458); and the belief that sexually provocative behavior, taken beyond a certain point, generates contracts. In summary, Pinzeau asserts that there are no grounds for the "she asked for it" defense; furthermore, given that it is a myth that men find it particularly difficult to contain their sexual desires, she grants the women the right to sexual provocation – she asks aptly: "[W]hy should this behavior warrant any kind of aggressive response whatsoever?" (1989: 459). Other changes in the regulation of the crime of rape that have taken place in many legal systems confirm that those myths are steadily being

---

[19] English translation (by the author): "atrocious hatred, wild egoism and the vile spirit of revenge."

[20] A similar approach can be noted in Étienne de Greeff, *Amour et crimes d'amour* (from 1942).

rejected: the abolition of the requirement of active resistance, even at the risk of physical injury, to sustain a charge of rape; the recognition of marital rape; the ban on evidence about the sexual history of the victim in rape trials.

4.3 Conclusions

In general, the abolition of the institution of "crimes of passion", or at least its very narrow/restrictive interpretation (recognizing their occurrence only in really exceptional cases), would be in accordance with the personalist picture of human beings: The picture implies the cognitive theory of emotions, according to which our emotions are to a very large extent controllable, so that there are no grounds for arguing that those who committed crimes of passion, unlike criminals committing "non-passionate" crimes, could not act otherwise. Another argument for the abolition of crimes of passion is that this institution is easily abused: Many defendants falsely claim, hoping to obtain a milder verdict, that they committed crimes in the heat of passion (cf. Sass 1983). However, it can hardly be denied that some counter-arguments could also be advanced. One could, e.g., point to various, subtle differences between "sins" committed through passion and those committed through malice, which could substantiate their different moral evaluation. Let me apologize for the long quote but Thomas Aquinas described these differences with unsurpassable clarity and perspicacity:

> A sin committed through malice is more grievous than a sin committed through passion, for three reasons. First, because, as sin consists chiefly in an act of the will, it follows that, other things being equal, a sin is all the more grievous, according as the movement of the sin belongs more to the will. Now when a sin is committed through malice, the movement of sin belongs more to the will, which is then moved to evil of its own accord, than when a sin is committed through passion, when the will is impelled to sin by something extrinsic, as it were. Wherefore a sin is aggravated by the very fact that it is committed through certain malice, and so much the more, as the malice is greater; whereas it is diminished by being committed through passion, and so much the more, as the passion is stronger. Secondly, because the passion which incites the will to sin, soon passes away, so that man repents of his sin, and soon returns to his good intentions; whereas the habit, through which a man sins, is a permanent quality, so that he who sins through malice, abides longer in his sin. For this reason the Philosopher (Ethic. vii, 8) compares the intemperate man, who sins through malice, to a sick man who suffers from a chronic disease, while he compares the incontinent man, who sins through passion, to one who suffers intermittently. Thirdly, because he who sins through certain malice is ill-disposed in respect of the end itself, which is the principle in matters of action; and so the defect is more dangerous than in the case of the man who sins through passion, whose purpose tends to a good end, although this purpose is interrupted on account of the passion, for the time being. Now the worst of all defects is defect of principle. Therefore it is evident that a sin committed through malice is more grievous than

one committed through passion. ... It is one thing to sin while choosing, and another to sin through choosing. For he that sins through passion, sins while choosing, but not through choosing, because his choosing is not for him the first principle of his sin; for he is induced through the passion, to choose what he would not choose, were it not for the passion. On the other hand, he that sins through certain malice, chooses evil of his own accord ..., so that his choosing, of which he has full control, is the principle of his sin: and for this reason he is said to sin "through" choosing (*Summa Theologiae*, II-I, q. 78, art. 4).

However, as can be inferred from this passage, most of the criteria which justify different moral evaluation of sins committed through passion and sins committed through malice (e.g., connection with will, disposition towards moral principles, the occurrence of sincere repentance) require the knowledge of the agent's mental states (which may not be transparent even to himself); their presence or absence cannot therefore be affirmed with any certainty. For this reason, they should be taken into account only within the "cosmic/God's eyes" conception of responsibility – the conception which should not guide the work of a legislator.

Epilogue

The philosophical basis of this book was the personalist view of human beings. I have provided several philosophical arguments in its favor, but one can add in this place also a pragmatic one, viz. there are some empirical findings which demonstrate that disbelief in free will (a crucial part of this view) leads to increased aggression, to increased tendency to lie and cheat, to decreased willingness to help others, and to conformist behavior (cf. Baumeister 2010). This pragmatic argument is obviously controversial and, even if true, of secondary importance; nonetheless it is undoubtedly worth mentioning. I have argued that several important consequences flow from the personalist view with regard to the insanity defense. The first of them is a conception of responsibility based on the requirement of free will. This is a natural consequence: If we assume a view of human being which implies that they are endowed with free will, then it would be odd not to accept the conception of responsibility which, arguably, provides its (responsibility's) best justification. Yet the conception endorsed by the personalist picture is not blind to the fact that free will can be suspended due to an internal coercion caused by mental illness. Thus, the personalist picture leads to the Standard Model of criminal responsibility (Mentally sane → Responsible; Mentally ill → Not-responsible). Furthermore, the personalist view of human beings leads by two routes to skepticism towards the volitional component. The first route is the fact that it implies a strong presumption in favor of the effectiveness of will. Will is a central feature of person and it can only be deemed ineffective in exceptional circumstances. The second route is the fact that will can be developed. The mere presence of a liberally (broadly) interpreted volitional (insanity) defense might exert a negative, motivational effect: It would discourage people from working on the development of their will, both decisional and post-decisional. It would therefore constitute one of those cultural factors which, more or less openly, permit or condone volitional failures. In summary, if we deem the personalist view correct, we must reject the liberal – broad – understanding of the volitional component: The two are simply irreconcilable. Since the personalist view of human being is inextricably connected with the cognitive theory of emotions, it also leads to skepticism towards the crimes of passion. Furthermore, I have argued that the cognitive component is to be understood in a narrow manner – as requiring, in order to ascribe responsibility to the agent, his mere knowledge (not "appreciation") of the nature and quality of the act and of the distinction between right and wrong. The basic argument for this claim was that there are many types of moral reasons, some of which can be grasped even by people with affective/emotional deficits. In general, the postulates advocated in this book amount to the requirement to set the threshold for a successful insanity defense at a high level. These postulates are largely realized in common law systems but not in continental legal systems, where a liberal construction of the insanity defense (including both components – the cognitive and the volitional – and each of them being understood broadly) is still dominant.

Bibliography

Arendt, Hannah (1978) *Willing*, in: H. Arendt, *The Life of the Mind*, San Diego, CA, New York, NY, London: Harcourt Brace Jovanovich.
Aristotle (1947) *Nicomachean Ethics*, transl. W.D. Ross, New York, NY: The Modern Library.
Baron-Cohen, Simon (1995) *Mindblindness: An Essay on Autism and Theory of Mind*, Cambridge, MA: MIT Press.
Baron-Cohen, Simon (2011) *The Science of Evil: On Empathy and the Origins of Cruelty*, New York, NY: Basic Books.
Basaglia, Franco (ed.) (1973) *L'Istituzione Negata*, Turin: Einaudi.
Baumeister, Roy F. (2001) *Evil. Inside Human Violence and Cruelty*, New York, NY: Henry Holt and Company.
Baumeister, Roy F. (2010) 'Understanding Free Will and Consciousness on the Basis of Current Research Findings in Psychology', in: R. Baumeister, A.R. Mele, K.D. Vohs (eds.), *Free Will and Consciousness. How Might They Work?*, Oxford: Oxford University Press, pp. 24–43.
Baumeister, Roy F., Heatherton, Todd F. (1996) 'Self-regulation Failure: An Overview', *Psychological Inquiry*, 7(1), pp. 1–15.
Baumeister, Roy F., Vohs, Kathleen. D. (2007) 'Self-Regulation, Ego Depletion, and Motivation', *Social and Personality Psychology Compass*, 1(1), pp. 115–128.
Black, Donald (1983) 'Crime as Social Control', *American Sociological Review*, 48(1), ss. 34–45.
Blair, Robert J.R. (1995) 'A Cognitive Developmental Approach to Morality: Investigating the Psychopath', *Cognition* 57, pp. 1–29.
Blair, Robert J.R. (1997) 'Moral Reasoning and the Child with Psychopathic Tendencies', *Personality and Individual Differences*, 26, pp. 731–739.
Blair, Robert J.R. (2008) 'The Cognitive Neuroscience of Psychopathy and Implications for Judgments of Responsibility', *Neuroethics* 1, pp. 149–157.
Bradley, Francis H. (1894) 'Some Remarks on Punishment', *International Journal of Ethics*, 4, pp. 269–284.
Brooks, Alexander D. (1985) 'The Merits of Abolishing the Insanity Defense', *The Annals of the American Academy of Political and Social Science*, 477, pp. 125–136.
Cassirer, Ernst (1972, 1944) *An Essay on Man. An Introduction to a Philosophy of Human Culture*, New Haven, CT and London: Yale University Press.
Cirincione, Carmen, Jacobs, Charles (1999) 'Identifying Insanity Acquittals: Is It Any Easier?' *Law and Human Behavior*, 23, pp. 487–497.
Cooper, David (1967) *Psychiatry and Anti-Psychiatry*, London: Tavistock.
Daly, Martin, Wilson, Margot (2008, 1998) *Homicide*, New Brunswick, NJ: Transaction Publishers.
Donohue, Andrew, Arya, Vinay, Fitch, Lawrence, Hammen, Debra (2008) 'Legal Insanity: Assessment of the Inability to Refrain', *Psychiatry*, 5(3), pp. 58–66.
Duff, Anthony (1977) 'Psychopathy and Moral Understanding', *American Philosophical Quarterly*, 14, pp. 189–200.

Dworkin, Ronald (2011) *Justice for Hedgehogs*, Cambridge, MA: Belknap Press.
Elliott, Carl (1996) *The Rules of Insanity: Moral Responsibility and the Mentally Ill Offender*, Albany, NY: SUNY.
Ellis, James W., Luckasson, Ruth A. (1985) 'Mentally Retarded Criminal Defendants', *George Washington Law Review*, 53(414), pp. 414–493.
Erickson, Patricia E., Erickson, Steven K. (2008) *Crime, Punishment, and Mental Illness*, New Brunswick, NJ: Rutgers University Press.
Eshleman, Andrew (2016) 'Moral Responsibility', The Stanford Encyclopedia of Philosophy (Winter 2016 edition), Edward N. Zalta (ed.), https://plato.stanford.edu/archives/win2016/entries/moral-responsibility/>
Feinberg, Joel (2002a) 'Evil', in: J. Feinberg, *Problems at the Roots of Law: Essays in Legal and Political Theory*, Oxford: Oxford University Press, pp. 125–192.
Feinberg, Joel (2002b) 'Fusion', in: J. Feinberg, *Problems at the Roots of Law: Essays in Legal and Political Theory*, Oxford: Oxford University Press, pp. 193–200.
Ferri, Enrico (2004, 1893) *La sociologie criminelle (Sociologia criminale)*, Editions Dalloz-Sirey.
Fields, Lloyd (1996) 'Psychopathy, Other-Regarding Moral Beliefs, and Responsibility', *Philosophy, Psychiatry, and Psychology*, 3, pp. 261–277.
Fingarette, Herbert (1972) *The Meaning of Criminal Insanity*, Berkeley, CA: University of California Press.
Fingarette, Herbert (1974) 'Diminished Mental Capacity as a Criminal Law Defense', *The Modern Law Review*, 37(3), pp. 264–280.
Fingarette, Herbert (1976) 'Disabilities of Mind and Criminal Responsibility – A Unitary Doctrine', *Columbia Law Review*, 76(2), pp. 236–266.
Fingarette, Herbert (1985) 'The Disability of Mind Doctrine', *The Annals of the American Academy of Political and Social Science*, 477, pp. 104–113.
Fischer, John M., Ravizza, Mark (1998) *Responsibility and Control: A Theory of Moral Responsibility*, New York, NY: Cambridge University Press.
Foucault, Michel (1971, 1961) *Madness and Civilization (*Histoire de la folie à l'âge classique*)*, transl. R. Howard, London: Tavistock.
Geis, Gilbert, Meier, Robert F. (1985) 'Abolition of the Insanity Plea in Idaho: A Case Study', *The Annals of the Amercian Academy of Political and Social Science*, 477, pp. 72–83.
Gilson, Étienne (1958, 1948) *Duch filozofii średniowiecznej (L'esprit de la philosophie medieval)*, transl. J. Rybałt, Warsaw: PAX.
Glannon, Walter (1997) 'Psychopathy and Responsibility', *Journal of Applied Philosophy*, 14, pp. 263–275.
Glannon, Walter (2008) 'Moral Responsibility and the Psychopath', *Neuroethics*, 1, pp. 158–166.
Glover, Jonathan (1970) *Responsibility*, New York, NY: Humanities.
Goffman, Erving (1961) *Asylums. Essays on the Social Situation of Mental Patients and Other Inmates*, New York, NY: Random House.
Goldstein, Joseph, Katz, Jay (1963) 'Abolish the "Insanity Defense" – Why Not?', *Yale Law Journal*, 72(5), pp. 853–876.
de Greeff, Étienne (1942) *Amour et crimes d'amour*, Brussels: Editions Charles Dessart.
Hage, Jaap (2020) 'Brains, Minds, Responsibility, and Liability', http://www.jaaphage.nl/pdf/BrainMindResponsibility.pdf.
Haji, Ishtiyaque (1998) 'On Psychopaths and Culpability', *Law and Philosophy*, 17, pp. 117–140.

Haji, Ishtiyaque (2003) 'The Emotional Depravity of Psychopaths and Culpability', *Legal Theory*, 9(1), pp. 63–82.
Haji, Ishtiyaque (2010) 'Psychopathy, Ethical Perception, and Moral Culpability', *Neuroethics*, 3, pp. 135–150.
Hampton, Jean (1992) 'An Expressive Theory of Retribution', in: W. Cragg (ed.), *Retributivism and Its Critics*, Stuttgart: Franz Steiner, pp. 1–25.
Hart, Herbert L.A. (2008, 1968) *Punishment and Responsibility*, Oxford: Oxford University Press.
Holton, Richard (2010) 'Disentangling the Will', in: R. Baumeister, A.R. Mele, K.D. Vohs (eds.), *Free Will and Consciousness. How Might They Work?*, Oxford: Oxford University Press, pp. 82–100.
Hotchkiss, Sandy, Masterson, James F. (2003) *Why Is It Always About You? The Seven Deadly Sins of Narcissism*, New York, NY: Free Press.
Hume, David (1998, 1751) *An Enquiry Concerning the Principles of Morals*, Oxford: Oxford University Press.
Kendell, Robert E. (2005) 'The Myth of Mental Illness', in: J. Schaler (ed.), *Szasz Under Fire: The Psychiatric Abolitionist Faces His Critics*, Chicago, IL: Open Court, pp. 29–48.
Kenny, Anthony (2012) *Freewill and Responsibility*, London: Routledge.
Kępiński, Antoni (1974) *Schizofrenia*, Warsaw: Państwowy Zakład Wydawnictw Lekarskich.
Kotowicz, Zbigniew (1997) *R.D. Laing and the Paths of Anti-Psychiatry*, London and New York, NY: Routledge.
Laing, Ronald D. (1967) *The Politics of Experience and the Bird of Paradise*, Harmondsworth: Penguin Books.
Laing, Ronald D. (1969, 1960) *The Divided Self. An Existential Study in Sanity and Madness*, Harmondsworth: Penguin Books.
Laing, Ronald D. (1985) *Wisdom, Madness and Folly. The Making of a Psychiatrist*, London: Macmillan.
Lewis, Clive S. (1943) *The Abolition of Man*, Oxford: Oxford University Press.
Lewis, Clive S. (1954) 'The Humanitarian Theory of Punishment', *Res Judicatae*, 6, pp. 224–230.
Lewis, Clive S. (2009, 1952) *Mere Christianity*, New York, NY: HarperCollins.
Litton, Paul (2008) 'Responsibility Status of the Psychopath: On Moral Reasoning and Rational Self-Governance', *Rutgers Law Journal*, 39, pp. 350–392.
Lombroso, Cesare (1991, 1896) *La femme criminelle et la prostituée*, Editions Jérome Million.
Lorenz, Konrad (1996, 1983) *Tak zwane zło (Das Sogenannte Böse. Zur Naturgeschichte der Aggression*) transl. A.D. Tauszyńska, Warsaw: PIW.
Maibom, Heidi L. (2008) 'The Mad, the Bad, and the Psychopath', *Neuroethics*, 1, pp. 167–184.
Marcinkowska-Rosół, Maria (2018) 'The Concept of Brutishness (*THĒRIOTĒS*) in Aristotle's *Nicomachean Ethics*', *Roczniki humanistyczne*, 66(3), pp. 82–117.
Menninger, Karl (1963) *The Vital Balance*, New York, NY: Viking.
Menninger, Karl (2007, 1968) *The Crime of Punishment*, Bloomington, IN: AuthorHouse.
Moore, Michael S. (1984) *Law and Psychiatry: Rethinking the Relationship*, Cambridge: Cambridge University Press.
Morse, Stephen J. (2002) 'Uncontrollable Urges and Irrational People', *Virginia Law Review*, 5(88), pp. 1054–1063.

Morse, Stephen J. (2008a) 'Psychopathy and Criminal Responsibility', *Neuroethics*, 1, pp. 205–212.
Morse, Stephen J. (2008b) 'Determinism and the Death of Folk Psychology: Two Challenges to Responsibility from Neuroscience', *The* Minnesota *Journal of Law, Science & Technology*, 9(1), pp. 1–36.
Mounier, Emmanuel (1936) *Manifeste au service du personnalisme*, Editions Montaigne, Paris: Fernand Aubier.
Murphy, Jeffrie G. (1972) 'Moral Death: A Kantian Essay on Psychopathy', *Ethics*, 82(4), pp. 284–298.
Nevins-Saunders, Elisabeth (2012) 'Not Guilty as Charged: The Myth of Mens Rea for Defendants with Mental Retardation', *University of California, Davis Law Review*, 45, pp. 1419–1486.
Nichols, Shaun (2002) 'How Psychopaths Threaten Moral Rationalism: Is It Irrational to Be Amoral?', *Monist*, 85, pp. 285–304.
Nisbett, Eichard E., Cohen, Dov (1996) *Culture of Honor. The Psychology of Violence in the South*, Boulder, CO: Westview Press.
Nozick, Robert (1990) *The Examined Life: Philosophical Meditations*, New York, NY: Simon & Schuster.
Patrick, Christopher J., Fowles, D.C., Krueger, R.F. (2009) 'Triarchic Conceptualization of Psychopathy: Developmental Origins of Disinhibition, Boldness, and Meanness', *Development and Psychopathology*, 21, pp. 913–938.
Pico della Mirandola, Giovanni (2010) *Oratio de hominis dignitate*, Warsaw: Wydawnictwo IFiS PAN (English translation: *Oration on the Dignity of Man*, transl. A. Robert Caponigri, Chicago, IL: Henry Regnery Company, 1956).
Pieper, Josef (2001, 1977) *The Concept of Sin (Über den Begriff der Sünde)*, transl. E.T. Oakes, South Bend, IN: St. Augustine's Press.
Pinker, Steven (2011) *The Better Angels of Our Nature. Why Violence Has Declined*, New York, NY: Viking Books.
Pinzeau, Lois (1989) 'Date Rape: A Feminist Analysis', *Law and Philosophy*, 8(2), pp. 217–243.
Posner, Eric A. (2000) 'Law and the Emotions', *University of Chicago Law & Economics, Olin Working Paper No. 103*, https://chicagounbound.uchicago.edu/law_and_economics/303/.
Prinz, Jesse (2007) *The Emotional Construction of Morals*, Oxford: Oxford University Press.
Rabinowicz, Léon (1931) *Le Crime Passionnel*, Paris: Editions Rivière.
Reznek, Lawrie (1997) *Evil or Ill? Justifying the Insanity Defence*, London and New York, NY: Routledge.
Robertson, John (2001) 'Internalism, Practical Reason, and Motivation', in: E. Millgram (ed.), *Varieties of Practical Reasoning*, Cambridge, MA and London: The MIT Press, pp. 127–152.
Robinson, Daniel (1996) *Wild Beasts and Idle Humours. The Insanity Defense from Antiquity to the Present*, Cambridge MA and London, Harvard University Press.
Rops, Daniel (1962, 1948) *Wola (Vouloir. Réflexions sur la volonté)*, transl. M. Ponińska, Warsaw: Pax.
Rosen, George (1968) *Madness in Society. Chapters in the Historical Sociology of Mental Illness*, Chicago, IL and London: The University of Chicago Press.
Ross, Alf (1975) *On Guilt, Responsibility, and Punishment*, Berkeley, CA and Los Angeles, CA: University of California Press.
Ryle, Gilbert (1976) *The Concept of Mind*, Harmondsworth: Penguin Books.

Sass, Henning (1983) 'Affektdelikte', *Nervenarzt*, 54, pp. 557–572.
Scheff, Thomas (1984) *Being Mentally Ill: A Sociological Theory*, New York, NY: Harper & Row.
Scheler, Max (2014, 1913) *Der Formalismus in der Ethik und die matierale Wertethik. Neuer Versuch der Grundlegung eines ethischen Personalismus*, Hamburg: Felix Meiner Verlag.
Schmidt-Salomon, Michael (2012, 2005) *Humanizm ewolucyjny (Manifest des evolutionären Humanismus)*, transl. A. Lipiński, Słupsk: Wydawnictwo Dobra Literatura.
Schopp, Robert, F. (1991) *Automatism, Insanity, and the Psychology of Criminal Responsibility. A Philosophical Inquiry*, Cambridge: Cambridge University Press.
Searle, John (2010) 'Consciousness and the Problem of Free Will', in: R. Baumeister, A.R. Mele, K.D. Vohs (eds.), *Free Will and Consciousness. How Might They Work?*, Oxford: Oxford University Press, pp. 121–134.
Seneca (2020) *Of Clemency*, wikisource.
Shorter, Edward (2011) 'Still Tilting at Windmills: Commentary on *The Myth of Mental Illness*', *The Psychiatrist*, 35(5), pp. 183–184.
Siegler, Miriam, Osmond, Humphry, Mann, Harriet (1969) 'Laing's Models of Madness', *The British Journal of Psychiatry*, 115(525), pp. 947–958.
Silberman, Charles E. (1978) *Criminal Violence, Criminal Justice*, New York, NY: Vintage.
Sorabji, Richard (2000) *Emotion and Peace of Mind: From Stoic Agitation to Christian Temptation*, Oxford: Clarendon Press.
Strawson, Galen (1994) 'The Impossibility of Moral Responsibility', *Philosophical Studies*, 75(1–2), pp. 5–24.
Strawson, Peter (1962) 'Freedom and Resentment', in: G. Watson (ed.), Proceedings of the British Academy, Volume 48, Oxford: Oxford University Press, pp. 1–25.
Sykes, Charles J. (1993) *A Nation of Victims: The Decay of the American Character*, New York, NY: Saint Martin's Press.
Szasz, Thomas (1963) *Law, Liberty and Psychiatry: An Inquiry into the Social Uses of Mental Health Practices*, New York, NY: Syracuse University Press.
Szasz, Thomas (1974, 1960) *The Myth of Mental Illness: Foundations of a Theory of Personal Conduct*, New York, NY: Harper & Row.
Szasz, Thomas (1976) 'Anti-Psychiatry: The Paradigm of a Plundered Mind', *New Review*, 3(29), pp. 3–14.
Szasz, Thomas (1980) '"J'accuse": Psychiatry and the Diminished Capacity for Justice', *The Journal of Mind and Behavior*, 1(1), pp. 111–120.
Szasz, Thomas (1990) 'Law and Psychiatry: The Problem That Will Not Go Away', *The Journal of Mind and Behavior*, 11(3/4), pp. 557–563.
Szasz, Thomas and others (1996) 'Should the Insanity Defense Be Abolished?' (debate), http://www.szasz.com/insanity.pdf.
Szasz, Thomas (2011) 'The Myth of Mental Illness: 50 Years Later', *The Psychiatrist*, 35(5), pp. 179–182.
Thomas Aquinas. *Summa Theologiae*, https://www.corpusthomisticum.org/. English translation by Fathers of the English Dominican Province, https://www.doc umentacatholicaomnia.eu/03d/1225-1274,_Thomas_Aquinas,_Summa_Theologiae _%5b1%5d,_EN.pdf.
Torrey, E. Fuller (1997) *Out of the Shadows. Confronting America's Mental Illness*, London: Wiley.
Toure, Habiba (2007) *Le crime passionnel* (PhD Thesis), https://static.mediapart.fr/files/ToureThese.pdf.

Turiel, Elliot (1979) 'Distinct Conceptual and Developmental Domains: Social Convention and Morality', in: H. Howe, C. Keasey (eds.), *Nebraska Symposium on Motivation, 1977: Social Cognitive Development*, Lincoln, NE: University of Nebraska Press.
Turiel, Elliot (1983) *The Development of Social Knowledge*, Cambridge: Cambridge University Press.
Turiel, Elliot, Nucci, Larry P. (1978) 'Social Interactions and the Development of Social Concepts in Preschool Children', *Child Development*, 49, pp. 400–407.
Twardowski, Kazmierz (1983) 'Etyka i prawo karne wobec zagadnienia wolności woli', *Etyka*, 20, pp. 123–157.
Vallacher, Robin R., Wegner, Daniel W. (1987) 'What Do People Think They Are Doing? Action Identification and Human Behaviour', *Psychological Review*, 94(1), pp. 3–15.
Vallacher, Robin R., Wegner, Daniel W. (2012) 'Action Identification Theory', in: P.A.M Van Lange, A.W. Kruglanski, E.T. Higins (eds.), *Handbook of Theories of Social Psychology, Vol. I*, London: Sage Publications, pp. 327–348.
Vincent, Nicole A. (2011) 'Neuroimaging and Responsibility Assessments', *Neuroethics*, 4(1), pp. 35–49.
Wakefield, Jerome C. (1992) 'The Concept of Mental Disorder: On the Boundary Between Biological Facts and Social Values', American Psychologist, 47(3), pp. 373–388.
Ward, Mary Jane (1947) *The Snake Pit*, London: Random House.
Wojtyła, Karol (John Paul II) (1985, 1960) *Miłość i odpowiedzialność*, Lublin: Towarzystwo Naukowe KUL.
Wojtyła, Karol (John Paul II) (1986a) 'Zagadnienie woli w analizie aktu etycznego', in: K. Wojtyła, *Zagadnienie podmiotu moralności*, Lublin: Towarzystwo Naukowe KUL, pp. 181–200.
Wojtyła, Karol (John Paul II) (1986b) 'O kierowniczej lub służebnej roli rozumu w etyce na tle poglądów św. Tomasza z Akwinu, Hume'a i Kanta', in: K. Wojtyła, *Zagadnienie podmiotu moralności*, Lublin: Towarzystwo Naukowe KUL, pp. 213–230.
Wojtyła, Karol (John Paul II) (2000, 1969) *Osoba i czyn*, Lublin: Towarzystwo Naukowe KUL.
Wootton, Barbara (1960) 'Diminished Responsibility: A Layman's View', *Law Quarterly Review*, 76, pp. 224–239.
Wootton, Barbara (1963) *Crime and the Criminal Law*, London: Steven & Sons.
Załuski, Wojciech (2018) *Law and Evil: The Evolutionary Perspective*, Cheltenham: Edward Elgar Publishing.
Załuski, Wojciech (2017) 'Naturalism as the Suicide of Thought', Polish Law Review, 3(1), pp. 215-229.
Zaremba, Maciej (2008) 'Sceny łowieckie z domu wariatów', transl. W. Chudoba, in: M. Zaremba, *Polski hydraulik i inne opowieści ze Szwecji*, wydawnictwo czarne, Wołowiec, pp. 175–229.

Index

actus reus 26–28, 51, 53, 68
animal rationale 6
Affluenza Defense 117–118
akrasia 109
anti-psychiatry 13, 34–35, 42–44, 46–47, 56–57, 59, 61, 64
appetitus intellectivus vs. *sensitivus* 103–105
Arendt, Hannah 103–105, 108–109, 111
Aristotle 25, 96–97, 101, 109
Arya, Vinay 120
St. Augustine of Hippo 94, 106, 109–110
Baron-Cohen, Simon 80
Basaglia, Franco 34, 59
Baumeister, Roy F 100–101, 115–117, 130
Bergson, Henri 111
Blair, Robert J.R. 78–80
Boethius 92, 107
St. Bonaventure 108
Bradley, Francis H. 28
Branting, Georg 55
Brooks, Alexander D. 51
Cassirer, Ernst 3
categorical imperative 86, 91, 102, 107
causa sui 23–25, 31, 48, 62, 111
Character Change Defense 121
Cirincione, Carmen 118
Cohen, Dov 117
Cooper, David 34, 47
crimes of passion 122–129
Daly, Martin 98–99
defectus
    naturalis vs. *culpae* 108
deific-decree doctrine 69
deinstitutionalization 56–59
delusions 19, 33, 69, 75–76, 86, 120–121
determinism 7, 21, 54, 66
    hard 21
Dostoyevsky, Fiodor 105
Duff, Anthony 81–82
Donohue, Andrew 120

Drummond, Edward 69
Duns Scotus 105, 120
the Durham rule (test) 18, 73–74
Dworkin Ronald 62–63
egotism 100
Elliott, Carl 81
Ellis, James W. 2, 19
emotions
    cognitive theory of 123–125, 128, 130
    non-cognitive theory of 123
empathy 40, 56, 77, 80–81, 86, 102
    affective 77, 80
    cognitive 77, 80
Erickson, Patricia E. 43, 52, 55–59, 113, 117
Erickson, Steven K. 43, 52, 55–59, 113, 117
Eshleman, Andrew 27
evil
    extreme 15, 75, 91–102
excuses (legal) 1
Feinberg, Joel 22, 94–95, 99, 101
Ferri, Enrico 48, 54–55, 126
Fields, Lloyd 82
Fingarette, Herbert 26–27, 30–31, 119
Fischer, John Martin 26
Fitch, Lawrence 120
folk psychology 106
Foucault, Michel 35–38
Fowles, Don C. 77
freedom of will (free will) 3–5, 7–14, 22, 24, 31, 42, 48, 50–51, 57, 62–63, 67, 87, 91, 93, 104, 106–110, 130
Geis, Gilbert 51–52
Gilson, Étienne 108–109
Glannon, Walter 81, 84
Glover, Jonathan 82, 84
Goffman, Erving 34
Goldstein, Joseph 41
de Greeff, Étienne 127
Hage, Jaap 32

Haji, Ishtiyaque 80
Hammen, Debra 120
Hampton, Jean 85
Hart, Herbert L. A. 28–31, 51, 53, 113–114, 118
Heatherton, Todd. F 115, 117
Hinckley, Jr, John W. 52, 72
Holton, Richard 77
humanism 7, 8
   evolutionary 8
   existentialist 8
   naturalistic 8
   personalist 10
   Promethean 8
Hume, David 25, 90–91
the insanity defense
   the concept of 1–2
   the history of 68–74
irresistible impulse 70–71, 73, 103, 113, 115–118, 120, 127
Jacobs, Charles 118
justifications (legal) 1–2
Justinian 48
Kant, Immanuel 90–91, 110
Katz, Jay 41
Kendell, Robert E. 64
Kenny, Anthony 70–71, 115, 119
Kesey, Ken 56
Kępiński, Antoni 76, 98, 118
Kotowicz, Zbigniew 38, 42, 46–47
Krueger, Robert F. 77
Laing, Ronald D. 44–47
Lewis, Clive S. 10–11, 90, 93–94
libertas
   minor vs. *major* 106–107
Litton, Paul 81, 83, 90
Lombroso, Cesare 126
low-level thinking 76, 82
Lorenz, Konrad 80
Luckasson, Ruth A. 2, 19
magnitude gap 101
Maibom, Heidi L. 85, 86
malum in se vs. *prohibitum* 14, 84–86
Mann, Harriet 38
Marcinkowska-Rosół, Maria 96
Meier, Robert F. 51–52
Menninger, Karl 21, 49–50
mens rea 26–32, 41, 51–53, 68, 77
mental competence to stand trial 2, 41, 51, 66

mental illness
   affirmative account of 13, 32–34, 63–65
   continuum/spectrum concept of 43, 60, 119
   Darwinian interpretation of 98–99
   negationist account of 13, 34–47, 63–65
mental retardation 2, 18–19
M'Naghten, Daniel 69
the M'Naghten rule 69, 70–72, 76, 102
the Model Penal Code 71–72, 76, 88
Moore, Michael, S. 1
moral cognitivism 90–91
moral externalism 88–89
moral internalism 88–89
moral sentimentalism 90
Morse, Stephen J. 26, 82, 84, 116
Mounier, Emmanuel 7–8
Murphy, Jeffrie G. 83, 94, 102
Nevins-Saunders, Elisabeth 118
Nichols, Shaun 90
Nisbett, Richard E. 117
Nozick, Robert 123
Nucci, Larry P. 79
Osmond, Humphrey 38
Patrick, Christopher. J. 77
St. Paul 105, 109
Peel, Robert 69
person 7–8, 107
personalist ethics 107
personalist view of human beings 2–8
Pico della Mirandola, Giovanni 3–4, 8, 10
Pieper, Josef 108
Pinker, Steven 77
Pinzeau, Lois 127
Plato 92
Posner, Eric A. 122, 124–125
Prinz, Jesse 80, 89–90
Prohairesis 25, 109
psychopaths
   solutions to the problem of their responsibility 14, 78–88
   their characteristics 77–78
punishment
   expressive theory of 85
   humanitarian theory of 92–94
   retributive theory of 31, 56, 67
Rabinowicz, Léon 126

rape
    legal approach to 127–128
rationality
    its relation to freedom of will 5–7
Ravizza Mark 26
Reagan, Ronald 52, 57
responsibility
    compatibilist conceptions of 25–32
    cosmic/God's eye view account of
        11, 14, 22, 87, 122, 129
    incompatibilist conceptions of
        21–25
    of the mentallly ill 16–19, 47–55,
        62–67
Reznek, Lawrie 18, 85, 102, 117–118,
    120–121
Robinson, Daniel 48, 50
Robertson, John 89
Rops, Daniel 103
Rosen, George 35, 48
Ross, Alf 27–28, 53, 55
rules
    conventional vs. moral 79–81,
        84–86
Ryle, Gilbert 111
Sartre, Jean Paul 8
Sass, Henning 128
Scheff, Thomas 39
Scheler, Max 60, 65, 110
Schlyter, Karl 55
Schmidt-Salomon, Michael 8
Searle, John 7
self-determination 3, 10, 15, 22–23, 107,
    110–111
self-possession 107
Seneca 95
Shorter, Edward 64
Siegler, Miriam 38
Silberman, Charles E. 21
Sorabji, Richard 109–110
spontaneity 104, 109
Strahl, Ivar 55
Strawson, Galen 23–24, 31, 111
Strawson, Peter 65–67
Sykes, Charles J. 49

Szasz, Thomas 35, 38–44, 47, 50, 57, 61,
    63–65
St. Thomas Aquinas 4–5, 7, 103, 105,
    108, 110, 120, 128
Theriotes 15, 96–97, 99
Torrey, E. Fuller 56, 58–61, 65
Toure, Habiba 126–127
transcendence
    capacity for 106, 110
    vertical 106
transistitutionalization 58–59
Turiel, Elliot 79
Twardowski, Kazmierz 25
Vallacher, Robin R. 76
Vincent, Nicole A. 78–79
vis
    bsoluta 9, 22
    compulsive 9, 22
Vohs, Kathleen 115
volitional component of the insanity
    defense
    the epistemic objection to 113–115
    the non-existence objection to
        115–117
    the slippery slope and the threat
        to formal justice objection
        117–118
volitional theory of action 105–106
Wakefield, Jerome C. 32–33, 64–65
Ward, May Jane 56
Wegner, Daniel W. 76
the "wild beast" test 69
will
    as a decisional power 103–111
    as a post-decisional power 111–112
    history of the concept of 108–111
    the unity of 112
Wilson, Margot 98–99
William of Ockham 105
Wojtyła, Karol (John Paul II) 90,
    106–107, 110
Wootton, Barbara 26–31, 113–114
Załuski, Wojciech 6, 94
Zaremba, Maciej 54–55